BAKE AND DESTROY

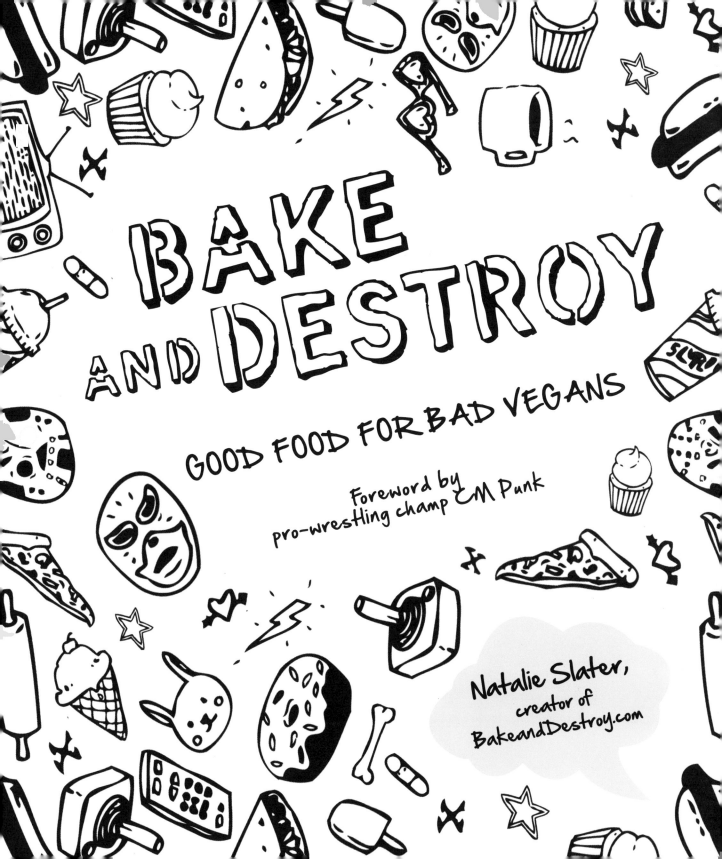

BAKE AND DESTROY

GOOD FOOD FOR BAD VEGANS

Foreword by
pro-wrestling champ CM Punk

Natalie Slater,
creator of
BakeandDestroy.com

PAGE STREET
PUBLISHING CO.

First published in 2013 by
Page Street Publishing
27 Congress Street, Suite 205-6
Salem, MA 01970
www.pagestreetpublishing.com

Distributed by Macmillan; sales in Canada by The Canadian Manda Group; distribution in Canada by The Jaguar
Book Group.

16 15 14 13 1 2 3 4 5

ISBN-13: 978-1-62414-002-0
ISBN-10: 1-624-14002-5

Library of Congress Control Number: 2013931989

Cover and book design by Page Street Publishing
Cover and border illustrations by Kristina and Amanda Bourlotos
Photography by Celine Steen
Photos on page 10 and 192 by Sean Dorgan
Photo on page 8 courtesy of WWE, Inc.
Illustrations by Agnes Barton-Sabo

Printed and bound in China

Dedicated to my dad—
chili cook-off champion,
Hawaiian shirt enthusiast,
and all-around great guy.

Contents

Foreword

Okay, you bought a cookbook with a foreword written by a pro-wrestler. Why am I writing this? Well for one, Natalie Slater and I have been through hell and back with each other—and she knows all my secrets. So when she asked me to write this (threatened to reveal my secrets), I fell over myself to write it!

But really, she didn't actually have to twist my arm to get me to tell you the recipes you're about to feast your eyes upon are all delicious as well as vegan. It's simply the facts. A lot of these recipes have been battle-tested by carloads of angry, 250-pound, starving pro-wrestlers who, if you told them after eating any assortment of Natalie's delicious treats that these goodies were, in fact, vegan, they would beat you up. There's no way those fantastic brownies are vegan because pro-wrestlers don't eat "that crap."

Alas, most of the world still adheres to the fallacy that athletes cannot survive on a plant-based diet. I, along with the contents of these pages, am here to convince you otherwise. Plus, who can resist desserts named after pro-wrestlers, such as the Samoa Joe Cupcakes? And just try to resist the Cannibal Corpse Crock-Pot, I dare you!

Truth is, Natalie is extremely passionate about plant-based baking and cooking, and the recipes in this book are as rad as the author. She put the same amount of hard work and love into every page of this book as she did with the vegan goodies she gave me on my way out the door to another wrestling adventure over a decade ago, so I know they're good!

I'd stay longer and say many more nice things about Natalie and her cooking wizardry, but writing this has made me hungry. Time for me (and you) to dive into this book and whip up something friends and family will gladly devour—not a leftover in sight. Enjoy, or else!

—CM Punk

Introduction

When I was a kid, if I wasn't sitting too close to the TV with a Nintendo controller in my hand, you could find me in the kitchen with my mom. No matter how grown-up I got, the magic of turning a handful of ingredients into cake or pizza or pie was never lost on me, and it helped me to form a very DIY credo: *If you're hungry, you should cook yourself something.*

But cookbooks can be so bossy! Just a bunch of people telling you how to make the "best" cupcake and the "ultimate" cornbread. My natural aversion to being told what to do is exactly what inspired me to start *Bake and Destroy* in the first place. I wanted to inspire people to try new things in the kitchen with a no-holds-barred approach. Food tastes better when you have fun making it, so why stress over whether or not it's "perfect"?

For years I've shared dessert recipes on my blog, but after transitioning to a mostly plant-based diet, I started getting more and more questions about what I eat *besides* cookies and cupcakes, so in this book not only do I give you awesome dessert recipes, I've also collected recipes for the food I really eat—from tacos to casseroles to a dairy-free version of the birthday cake my mom made me every year for my entire life. There's vegan food inspired by my favorite music, restaurants and even a few pro-wrestlers. My hope is that these recipes encourage you to try something new—and to use what you've learned to create your own recipes.

So get in the kitchen, and let's get weird.

—Natalie

Natalie

WORLD CHAMPION CUPCAKES!

OOOH YEAH!

WINNER!

THE BEST

Chapter 1

Sweets & Treats

Sophia Loren once said, "Everything you see, I owe to spaghetti." I'm no Sophia Loren, but I feel the same way about cupcakes. They took me to the Food Network as a judge on *Cupcake Wars*, to the Cooking Channel where I demonstrated my award-winning Banana Bread French Toast Cupcake recipe on *The Perfect 3*, and now, they have brought me to you—which might be my most exciting adventure yet! So while I don't have Sophia's sweet bod, she never wrote a cookbook, so who cares? (Dang it. I just Googled and she wrote *two* cookbooks. I shake my fist at you, Sophia Loren!)

Since launching Bake and Destroy in 2006, I have made cupcakes inspired by everything from slasher films to Andrew W.K. and it only gets weirder and more delicious from there. In this chapter I've included my award-winning recipe as mentioned above; a chocolate, coconut and caramel cupcake inspired by pro wrestler Samoa Joe; and a handful of other easy-to-make and even easier-to-eat cupcakes.

I've also included an over-the-top cake named after my favorite late-night B-movie hostess, Rhonda Shear, and some from-scratch snack cakes that might look familiar, but they certainly don't taste like Mom didn't used to make. Along with those, you'll find whoopie pies that look like tiny burgers but taste like a banana split and a couple of homemade cake mixes that make it easy to whip up dessert in minutes.

Brownies made with flaxseeds? Cheesecake made from tofu? What sorcery is this? This is what I do, dudes. I can turn a handful of cashews and a can of coconut milk into dessert faster than you can say, "This is vegan." And you can do it, too—so c'mon, let's get some sugar into you before we all starve!

Banana Bread French Toast Cupcakes

If you've spoken to my mom lately, you might know that I won a Cooking Channel competition with this recipe. Inspired by a dish at Salt & Pepper Diner in Chicago, these moist cupcakes combine cinnamon, maple and banana for a breakfasty-dessert.

Makes 12 cupcakes

Ingredients

CUPCAKES:

½ cup (113 g) mashed overripe banana
1 ¼ cups (156 g) all-purpose flour
¼ teaspoon baking soda
1 teaspoon baking powder
1 teaspoon ground cinnamon
½ teaspoon salt
¾ cup (150 g) sugar
⅓ cup (80 ml) canola oil
⅔ cup (160 ml) rice or soy milk
1 teaspoon vanilla extract
½ teaspoon almond extract
½ cup (60 g) chopped, toasted walnuts

VEGAN MAPLE BUTTERCREAM FROSTING:

2 cups (250 g) confectioners' sugar
6 tablespoons (85 g) nonhydrogenated vegetable shortening
6 tablespoons (85 g) vegan margarine
2 tablespoons (40 g) pure maple syrup
½ teaspoon maple flavoring
Pinch of salt

Directions

Preheat your oven to 350°F (180°C) and line a twelve-cup muffin pan with paper liners.

Throw your mashed banana in a blender or just smash it with a fork.

Sift the flour, baking soda, baking powder, cinnamon, salt and sugar into a large bowl and mix well.

In a smaller bowl, whisk together the oil, rice milk, vanilla, almond extract and mashed banana.

Stir or fold the wet ingredients into the dry. Small lumps are fine. Finally, add the walnuts, folding gently.

Fill the liners two-thirds full. Bake for 20 to 22 minutes, or until the tops spring back when lightly touched. Let cool in the pan on a wire rack for 10 minutes, then remove from the pan and let cool completely before frosting.

To make the vegan maple buttercream frosting, beat all the ingredients together in a bowl until they're light and fluffy.

Samoa Joe Cupcakes

These cupcakes might be inspired by my favorite Girl Scout cookie—or they could be inspired by a six-foot-two, 280-pound professional wrestler. Take a bite and see which one comes to mind when the chocolaty, coconutty, caramelly goodness puts the Kokina Clutch on your mouth.

Makes 12 cupcakes

Ingredients

CUPCAKES:

1 ½ cups (187 g) all-purpose flour

1 cup (200 g) sugar

¼ cup (29 g) unsweetened cocoa powder

1 teaspoon baking soda

1 teaspoon salt

1 cup (235 ml) cold water

6 tablespoons (89 ml) canola oil

1 teaspoon vanilla extract

1 tablespoon (15 ml) apple cider vinegar

1 ½ cups (140 g) shredded coconut

1 batch Caramel Sauce (page 48)

SALTED CARAMEL-COCONUT BUTTERCREAM:

½ cup (113 g) vegan margarine

½ cup (113 g) unhydrogenated vegetable shortening

3 ½ cups (437 g) confectioners' sugar

½ teaspoon salt

½ teaspoon coconut flavoring

¾ cup (70 g) shredded coconut

CHOCOLATE DRIZZLE:

½ cup (85 g) vegan chocolate chips

1 tablespoon (14 g) unhydrogenated vegetable shortening

Directions

Preheat your oven to 350°F (180°C) and line a twelve-cup muffin tin with paper liners.

To make the cupcakes, in a large bowl, sift together the flour, sugar, cocoa powder, baking soda and salt. Stir in the water, oil, vanilla, and vinegar, and fill the prepared cups two-thirds full. Bake for 18 to 21 minutes, or until the tops spring back when lightly touched. Let cool in the pan for 10 minutes, then remove from the pan and let cool on a wire rack.

While the oven is still on, spread the 1 ½ cups (140 g) of shredded coconut on a rimmed baking sheet lined with parchment paper. Toast for 6 to 8 minutes, stirring once or twice, until toasted. Remove from the oven and let cool.

Use a chopstick or a straw to poke four or five small holes in each cooled cupcake. Reserving ¼ cup (60 ml) of caramel sauce to use in the buttercream, use a spoon to drizzle caramel sauce into the holes.

To make the buttercream, beat the margarine and shortening together until well combined. Gradually beat in the confectioners' sugar on low speed, then increase speed to medium and beat 3 minutes until fluffy. Add the reserved caramel sauce, salt and coconut flavoring and beat to incorporate. Fold in the shredded coconut.

To make the drizzle, set up a double boiler and melt the chocolate and shortening together. Transfer the mixture into a resealable plastic bag and set aside to cool for about 10 minutes.

Use a piping bag or offset spatula to pile the buttercream high on each cupcake. Dunk each cupcake, frosting side down, into the toasted coconut. Place the cupcakes on a sheet of waxed paper, snip the corner from the bag containing the chocolate and drizzle a zigzag of chocolate over the top of each cupcake. The chocolate will set up in a few minutes.

Peach Cobbler Cupcakes

When I was a kid, my whole family vacationed together—uncles, aunts and piles of rowdy cousins. On one particular outing, we jammed the whole family into a buffet-style restaurant in Branson, Missouri. We were about to be late to a Yo-Yo Ma performance, but my Uncle Jim refused to leave until they replenished the giant hotel pan full of peach cobbler. Ever since then, "peach cobbler" has been a running joke among all of us. This recipe is dedicated to Uncle Jim, who had his priorities straight.

Makes 12 cupcakes

Ingredients

¾ cup (94 g) all-purpose flour
¾ cup (75 g) cake flour
⅔ cup (134 g) sugar
1 tablespoon (9 g) cornstarch
1 ½ teaspoons baking powder
¾ teaspoon ground cinnamon
½ teaspoon salt
¼ teaspoon ground nutmeg
¼ teaspoon ground cardamom
½ cup + 2 tablespoons (150 ml) soy milk
⅓ cup (80 ml) canola oil
1 ½ teaspoons vanilla extract
½ teaspoon apple cider vinegar
1 ½ cups (255 g) roughly chopped peaches (fresh or frozen)

Directions

Preheat your oven to 350°F (180°C) and line a twelve-cup muffin tin with paper liners.

Sift together flours, sugar, cornstarch, baking powder, cinnamon, salt, nutmeg and cardamom. Stir in the soy milk, oil, vanilla and vinegar. Allow the batter to rest for 5 minutes, then fold in the peaches.

Fill each muffin cup two-thirds full and bake for 22 to 26 minutes, until the tops spring back when lightly touched. Let cool in the pan for 10 minutes, then transfer to a wire rack and let cool completely.

Party Tip: I love these cupcakes with a plop of Whipped Coconut Cream (page 49) with a pinch of cinnamon whipped in, or with maple buttercream frosting (see Banana Bread French Toast Cupcakes, page 14).

Frozen Lemonade Pie

Years ago, my mom would mix frozen lemonade concentrate with a half-gallon of vanilla ice cream, spoon it onto a piecrust and bask in the glory of my sister, brother and me shutting up long enough to gobble up every last bite. Eventually I won my husband's heart with that very pie, and I've re-created it here with a tart vanilla and lemon ice cream made with coconut milk, in a quick graham cracker crust.

Serves 8 to 10

Ingredients

CRUST:

1 ½ cups (375 g) finely ground graham cracker crumbs

⅓ cup (67 g) sugar

⅓ cup (76 g) vegan margarine, melted

ICE CREAM:

2 (13.3-ounce [403 ml]) cans coconut milk

1 cup (235 ml) frozen lemonade concentrate, thawed

½ cup (162 g) agave nectar

2 tablespoons (30 ml) vanilla extract

Zest of 1 organic lemon

Directions

Preheat your oven to 375°F (190°C).

To make the crust, mix the graham cracker crumbs, sugar and margarine until well combined. Press into a 9-inch (23 cm) pie pan and bake for 7 minutes. Let cool completely.

Use a whisk to mix all the ice-cream ingredients together, then follow the directions on your ice-cream maker to freeze it. If the ice cream is too soft to add to the pie shell at this point, scoop it into a lidded container and place in the freezer for 2 hours. Once it's set up, scoop the ice cream into the pie shell, smooth the top with an offset spatula or the back of a spoon, cover with plastic wrap and freeze until firm enough to slice.

Pinterest Pie

I hate Pinterest. It's a place where weird moms post their corny party ideas and it creeps me out. So when my friends all started going nutty over some magical "frozen banana ice cream" they saw on Pinterest, I got ready to delete them all from Facebook. But before I committed mass Facebook murder, I gave pureed frozen bananas a try and I'll be damned—they taste like ice cream. But I still think Pinterest is stupid, so I improved upon the original by adding creamy peanut butter and pie-ifying it.

Serves 8 to 10

Ingredients

CRUST:

1 ¾ cups (122 g) crushed pretzels

3 tablespoons (39 g) sugar

¼ cup (57 g) melted vegan margarine, (or ¼ cup [60 ml] canola oil + ½ teaspoon salt)

1 tablespoon (15 ml) soy milk

3 ounces (85 g) vegan dark chocolate

FILLING:

5 peeled, very ripe bananas, sliced into coins and frozen until solid

¾ cup (195 g) creamy peanut butter

2 ½ tablespoons (51 g) agave nectar

Directions

Preheat your oven to 350°F (180°C) and spray a 9-inch (23 cm) pie pan with cooking spray. In a medium-size bowl, combine the pretzel crumbs and sugar, drizzle in the margarine and mix, then gradually add the soy milk—the dough will be crumbly. Scoop the mixture into the pie pan and press into the sides and bottom. Bake for 8 to 10 minutes, then let cool before coating with the chocolate. Melt the chocolate using a double boiler, and pour the melted chocolate onto the cooled crust. Tilt the pan to coat the bottom; if you have extra, keep tilting the pan to get some chocolate on the sides, too. Set aside to cool and set up—you can also place the pan in the freezer to speed up the process.

Puree the bananas in a food processor until they resemble soft-serve ice cream (You may want to do this in two or three batches, depending on the size and power of your food processor). Add the peanut butter and agave and scoop into the prepared pie shell. Cover with plastic wrap and freeze until set up enough to slice into—about 2 hours.

BurgerTime Whoopie Pies

BurgerTime, for those of you who are too young to be reading this book; is an early '80s video game featuring Chef Peter Pepper's quest to assemble giant hamburgers by running over the ingredients while fighting off killer hot dogs, pickles and eggs. It's one of the stupidest, most fun video games ever made, and I honor it with this really goofy dessert—whoopie pies that look like burgers and taste like a chocolate-covered fruit salad.

Makes 12 large burgers

Ingredients

BUNS:

1 ⅔ cups (207 g) all-purpose flour
1 ½ teaspoons baking soda
½ teaspoon ground nutmeg
½ teaspoon salt
¼ cup (57 g) nonhydrogenated vegetable shortening
¼ cup (57 g) vegan margarine
¾ cup (150 g) sugar
½ cup (113 g) mashed, ripe banana (about 1 large banana)
1 teaspoon vanilla extract
½ teaspoon almond extract
1 ¼ cups (295 ml) soy milk
2 to 3 tablespoons (16 to 24 g) sesame seeds

CHOCOLATE "BEEF PATTY":

1 ⅓ cups (166 g) confectioners' sugar
½ cup (59 g) unsweetened cocoa powder, sifted
¼ cup (57 g) vegan margarine
¼ cup (57 g) nonhydrogenated vegetable shortening
3 tablespoons (45 ml) soy milk
1 teaspoon vanilla extract
½ teaspoon salt

"MUSTARD":

2 tablespoons (28 g) vegan margarine
2 tablespoons (28 g) nonhydrogenated vegetable shortening
1 cup (125 g) confectioners' sugar
1 tablespoon (15 ml) soy milk
1 teaspoon vanilla or banana extract
3 to 4 drops yellow food coloring

OTHER TOPPINGS:

1 cup (93 g) shredded coconut
3 or 4 drops green food coloring
Strawberries

Directions

Preheat your oven to 350°F (180°C) and spray your whoopie pie pans with cooking spray. If you don't have whoopie pie pans, simply line two cookie sheets with parchment paper.

Sift together the flour, baking soda, nutmeg and salt onto a sheet of waxed paper. In a large bowl, beat together the margarine, shortening and sugar. Start on low speed to combine the ingredients, then switch to medium-high for 3 minutes, until the mixture is fluffy.

Add the banana and the vanilla and almond extract and beat for 2 more minutes.

Add half of the flour mixture and half of the soy milk, and mix until combined. Then add the remaining flour mixture and soy milk and mix until combined.

Drop 1 heaping tablespoon (20 ml) of batter into each cavity of the whoopie pie pan, or onto a lined cookie sheet, leaving at least 2 inches (5 cm) between each one. Sprinkle the sesame seeds on top of half of the unbaked whoopie pies—these will be the top buns. Bake for 10 minutes, or until the tops spring back when lightly touched. Let cool in the pan for 10 minutes, then transfer to a wire rack to cool completely.

To make the "patty," beat together the margarine, shortening, confectioners' sugar and cocoa powder on low speed, increasing to medium, until the mixture is crumbly, about 1 minute. Add the soy milk, vanilla and salt, and beat on high speed until smooth, about 3 minutes. Scoop into a piping bag or resealable plastic bag and refrigerate until firm—about an hour.

To make the "mustard," beat together the margarine and shortening on medium for about 1 minute. Add the confectioners' sugar and beat on low speed until combined. Add the soy milk, vanilla, and enough drops of yellow food coloring for the mixture to resemble mustard. Beat until smooth, about 4 minutes. Scoop into a piping bag or resealable plastic bag and refrigerate until firm—about an hour.

To make "shredded lettuce," place the shredded coconut in a large resealable plastic bag, add a few drops of green food coloring, close the bag and shake until the color is distributed evenly.

Wash and slice the strawberries to make "tomato" slices.

To assemble, invert a whoopie pie without sesame seeds and pipe on the chocolate buttercream in a large circle, resembling a burger patty. Sprinkle with some green coconut, and top with two slices of strawberries. Pipe the "mustard" over the top of all of the other toppings in a zigzag pattern. Top with a sesame seed whoopie pie and press down lightly, so the ingredients ooze out just like a juicy burger.

Party Tip: Prepare the "buns" and toppings ahead of time and let your guests assemble their own burgers. Get creative with the toppings. Roll out taffy for cheese and chop up fruit jellies for onions.

Pistachio Whoopie Pies

Rather than using a traditional marshmallow filling, I fill these with pistachio buttercream—fancy!
I felt compelled to color the filling green. Skip that step, if you prefer.

Makes 24 whoopie pies

Ingredients

WHOOPIES:

1 ⅔ cups (207 g) all-purpose flour

⅔ cup (79 g) unsweetened cocoa powder

1 ½ teaspoons baking soda

½ teaspoon salt

¼ teaspoon ground cardamom

¼ cup (57 g) vegan margarine

¼ cup (57 g) unhydrogenated vegetable shortening

1 cup packed (225 g) dark brown sugar

¼ cup (60 g) blended silken tofu or vegan soy yogurt

1 teaspoon vanilla extract

1 ¼ cups (295 ml) soy milk

¼ cup (25 g) finely ground pistachios

FILLING:

¼ cup (57 g) vegan margarine

¼ cup (57 g) nonhydrogenated vegetable shortening

3 cups (375 g) confectioners' sugar

3 to 4 tablespoons (45 to 60 ml) soy milk

1 teaspoon vanilla extract

½ teaspoon salt

½ cup (50 g) finely ground pistachios

Green food coloring (optional)

Directions

Preheat your oven to 375°F (190°C) and line a baking sheet with parchment paper or use an actual whoopie pie pan.

To make the whoopie pies: In a small bowl, sift together the flour, cocoa powder, baking soda, salt and cardamom.

In a stand mixer fitted with a paddle attachment, beat together the margarine, shortening and brown sugar on low speed until mixed, and then beat for 3 more minutes on medium speed. (You could also do this with a handheld electric mixer.) Add the tofu and vanilla and beat for 2 more minutes.

Add half the flour mixture and half of the soy milk and beat on low speed until just incorporated. Add the remaining flour mixture and soy milk and beat until completely combined. Add the ground pistachios and stir to incorporate.

To make about two dozen 2-inch (5 cm) whoopie pies, drop the batter 1 tablespoon (15 ml) at a time onto a lined baking sheet, spacing them about 2 inches (5 cm) apart. I use a whoopie pie pan, which makes about sixteen larger whoopie pies.

Bake for 10 minutes, or until the whoopies spring back when lightly touched. Let cool in the pan on a wire rack for 5 minutes, then remove from the pans to cool completely.

To make the filling, in the bowl of a stand mixer, beat together the margarine and shortening just until mixed. Add the confectioners' sugar, beat on medium for about 1 minute, until the mixture is crumbly. Add the soy milk, vanilla and salt and beat on high speed until smooth, about 3 minutes. Add the food coloring now, if using. Stir in the pistachios.

To assemble: When the whoopies are cool, match them up as best you can. Plop a dollop of filling on the underside of one (I use a pastry bag to do this, but you don't have to) and sandwich it together with another whoopie.

Lemon Meringue-ish Pie Cupcakes

I was working on a Key lime pie cupcake recipe when I started to get frustrated with all the contradictory opinions on ingredients out there. Some people act like if you use any other lime besides a Key lime, your head will explode or something. I don't have time for all these weird lime prejudices, so I opted to do lemon meringue-ish instead. Lemons are lemons, am I right? This tangy lemon curd recipe was adapted from one by prolific vegan cookbook author, Bryanna Clark Grogan.

Makes 12 cupcakes

Ingredients

LEMON CURD:

½ cup (120 ml) freshly squeezed lemon juice (2 to 3 lemons)

¼ cup (60 ml) water

¾ cup (150 g) sugar

2 tablespoons (19 g) cornstarch

Pinch of salt

Zest of 1 organic lemon

2 tablespoons + 2 teaspoons (40 ml) plain full-fat soy milk

1 tablespoon (14 g) vegan margarine

CRUST:

1 ½ cups (375 g) graham cracker crumbs

2 tablespoons (26 g) sugar

⅓ cup (76 g) vegan margarine, melted

CUPCAKES:

1 cup (125 g) all-purpose flour

¾ cup (75 g) cake flour

1 teaspoon baking powder

½ teaspoon baking soda

½ teaspoon salt

Zest of 1 organic lemon

¾ cup (150 g) sugar

⅓ cup (80 ml) canola oil

1 cup (235 ml) soy milk

1 teaspoon lemon flavoring (see note)

½ teaspoon vanilla extract

TOPPING:

Whipped Coconut Cream (page 49)

Zest from 1 lemon

¼ teaspoon almond extract

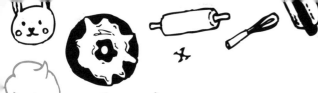

Directions

To make the lemon curd: In a food processor, combine the lemon juice, water, sugar, cornstarch and salt until smooth. Transfer to a saucepan and add the lemon zest. Over medium heat, whisk until the mixture comes to a full boil (about 10 minutes). You'll be standing there awhile, so this would be a good time to look through the rest of the book and start thinking about how many copies you want to order for your friends. Once boiling, stop stirring and let boil for 1 full minute. The mixture will be thick now.

Remove from the heat and whisk in the soy milk and margarine. Let cool in the pan until it reaches room temperature, then refrigerate in a closed container until ready to use.

Preheat your oven to 350°F (180°C) and line a twelve-cup muffin tin with paper liners.

For the crust, stir the graham cracker crumbs, sugar and margarine together. Place 1 tablespoon (15 g) of the mixture into the bottom of each prepared muffin cup. Use the bottom of a measuring cup or your fingers to pack the mixture into the bottom of each liner. Save the remaining crumbs for sprinkling later.

For the cupcakes, sift together the flours, baking powder, baking soda and salt. Stir in the lemon zest and sugar. In a large measuring cup, whisk together the oil, soy milk, lemon flavoring and vanilla. Stir the wet ingredients into the dry until just incorporated. Fill each liner two-thirds full and bake for 20 to 25 minutes, or until the tops spring back when lightly touched. Let cool in the pan for 10 minutes, then move to a wire rack to cool completely.

Fill the cupcakes: When the cupcakes are completely cool, use a small knife to cut a cone shape out of the center of each one—the top should be about 1 inch (2.5 cm) in diameter. You can discard the cones (I discard them into my mouth). Fill each hole with lemon curd—each one will hold about 1 ½ teaspoons.

Top each cupcake with a poof of Whipped Coconut Cream that has been beaten together with lemon zest and a touch of almond extract. Sprinkle with the remaining graham cracker crumbles.

Note: Lemon flavoring is more potent, not to mention more consistent, than fresh lemon juice. Look for an all-natural, alcohol-free flavor extract comprised mainly of lemon oil.

Party Tip: If you aren't a fan of coconut cream, top these cupcakes with a quick lemon buttercream. Beat together ¼ cup (57 g) of vegan margarine, ¼ cup (57 g) of unhydrogenated vegetable shortening, 1 ½ cups (187 g) of confectioners' sugar, and ¼ teaspoon of lemon flavoring. Pile it high and enjoy!

DIY Cake Mixes

Why buy a box of flour, sugar, baking soda and chemical stabilizers for a couple of bucks when you can make your own cake mix at home for pennies—no spooky chemicals required?

Chocolate Cake Mix

"Vinegar cake" was the first vegan recipe I learned when I was in high school. I used to make a version for CM Punk to share with the other wrestlers at indie wrestling shows. Like a boxed mix, this recipe makes enough batter for a 9 x 13-inch (23 x 33 cm) cake. See below for the bake times for different-size cakes.

Ingredients

DRY INGREDIENTS:

3 cups (375 g) all-purpose flour

2 cups (400 g) sugar

½ cup (59 g) unsweetened cocoa powder

2 teaspoons baking soda

2 teaspoons salt

LIQUID INGREDIENTS:

2 cups (475 ml) cold water

¾ cup (175 ml) oil

2 teaspoons vanilla extract

2 tablespoons (30 ml) apple cider vinegar

Directions

Sift the dry ingredients together into a large resealable plastic bag and store in a cool, dry place for up to 6 months.

Put the mix in a bowl and add the liquid ingredients. Stir well.

Pour into the prepared pan and bake at 350°F (180°C) for the following times:

- two 8-inch (20 cm) layers: 33 to 36 minutes
- two 9-inch (23 cm) layers: 28 to 31 minutes
- one 9 x 13-inch (23 x 33 cm) cake: 32 to 35 minutes
- one 10-inch (25.5 cm) Bundt cake: 38 to 43 minutes
- two dozen standard-size cupcakes: 18 to 21 minutes
- about six dozen mini cupcakes: 9 to 11 minutes

Vanilla Cake Mix

Consider this cake mix a canvas—dress it up with add-ins, such as sprinkles, spices or food coloring, or bake it in canoe pans for a homemade version of everyone's favorite cream-filled snack cake. The secret to this recipe is letting the batter rest—that extra time lets the baking powder get to work, producing a light and fluffy cake.

Ingredients

DRY INGREDIENTS:

1 ½ cups (187 g) all-purpose flour
1 ½ cups (150 g) cake flour
1 ½ cups (300 g) sugar
2 tablespoons (19 g) cornstarch
1 tablespoon (14 g) baking powder
1 teaspoon salt

LIQUID INGREDIENTS:

1 ¼ cups (295 ml) soy milk
⅔ cup (160 ml) oil
1 tablespoon (15 ml) vanilla extract
1 teaspoon apple cider vinegar

Directions

Sift the dry ingredients together into a large resealable plastic bag and store in a cool, dry place for up to 6 months.

Put the mix in a bowl and add the liquid ingredients. Stir well.

Allow the batter to rest for 5 minutes before pouring into prepared pan and baking at 350°F (180°C). See above for bake times.

Rhonda Shear's Up All Night Cake

If you stayed over at my house on a Friday night back in the day, you'd know I had two requirements for a good time—Mom's Better than Sex Cake, and *Up All Night with Rhonda Shear*. From 1991 to 1998, this B-movie goddess introduced me to such classics as *Attack of the Killer Tomatoes* and *Hell Comes to Frogtown*. This vegan version of BTS Cake is PG-13, but it's just naughty enough to be Rhonda-approved.

Serves 12 to 15

Ingredients

¾ cup (128 g) vegan semisweet chocolate

1 tablespoon (15 ml) soy milk

½ cup (55 g) slivered or chopped almonds

1 batch DIY Chocolate Cake Mix (page 31), baked in a 9 x 13-inch (23 x 33 cm) pan

½ batch Caramel Sauce (page 48)

1 batch Whipped Coconut Cream (page 49)

Directions

Cover a baking sheet with waxed paper. Place the chocolate and soy milk in a double boiler (see page 181), melting the chocolate. Stir in the almonds and spread the mixture onto the waxed paper. Chill in the refrigerator for about 20 minutes, or until the chocolate hardens. Remove from the fridge, and chop into small pieces.

With the handle of a wooden spoon, poke 2-inch (5 cm)-deep holes all over the cooled chocolate cake. Pour the caramel sauce into holes and drizzle on top of cake. Top with half of the chopped chocolate and frost with Whipped Coconut Cream. Sprinkle the top with the remaining chopped chocolate.

Chick-O-Cheesecake

Chick-O-Sticks are an old-school crunchy candy made with peanut butter and coconut. They are vegan, and even better, they're dirt cheap at most pharmacies and corner stores. I smashed them up for the a crust of this creamy peanut butter–coconut cheesecake.

Serves 8 to 10

Ingredients

CRUST:

1 cup (250 g) finely ground vegan graham crackers

¼ cup (37 g) finely crushed Chick-O-Stick candies

¼ teaspoon salt

2 tablespoons (30 ml) canola oil

1 tablespoon (15 ml) soy milk

FILLING:

½ cup (71 g) raw cashews

1 (12.3-ounce [349 g]) package silken tofu, drained

⅔ cup (134 g) sugar

2 tablespoons (18 g) light brown sugar

1 tablespoon (15 g) coconut oil, at room temperature, or coconut butter

¼ cup (37 g) cornstarch

2 teaspoons lemon juice

1 ½ teaspoons vanilla extract

½ teaspoon coconut flavoring

¼ teaspoon salt

1 cup (260 g) crunchy peanut butter

½ cup (46 g) shredded coconut

¼ cup (36 g) chopped peanuts

Crushed Chick-O-Sticks, for topping

Directions

Soak cashews in water until very soft, 2 to 8 hours.

Preheat your oven to 350°F (180°C) and spray a 9 ½-inch (24 cm) spring-form pan with cooking spray.

Make the crust: In a mixing bowl, combine the graham cracker crumbs, crushed Chick-O-Sticks and salt. Drizzle in 2 tablespoons (30 ml) of the oil, mixing well to moisten the crumbs. Add more oil gradually if needed. Add the soy milk, then press the dough into the bottom of the pan. Bake for 8 to 10 minutes until firm, and set aside to cool. Leave the oven on.

Make the filling: Drain the cashews and place in a food processor along with the tofu, sugar, brown sugar, coconut oil, cornstarch, lemon juice, vanilla, coconut flavoring and salt. Blend until smooth—there should be no chunks of cashew. Add the peanut butter and coconut and pulse to combine—this time there will be lumps of peanuts, and that's okay.

Pour the filling into the prepared crust, top with chopped peanuts (add a sprinkling of crushed Chick-O-Sticks, if desired) and bake on the top rack for 45 to 50 minutes, until the sides are golden and the top is puffy. To prevent a cracked surface, place a baking sheet on the lower rack, topped with an ovenproof dish containing 2 cups (475 ml) of hot water.

Remove the cheesecake from the oven and let it cool on a wire rack for 30 minutes, then refrigerate for at least 3 hours before slicing.

Bike Messenger Brownies

Every barista has a name for it: a chai latte with a couple of shots of espresso. Some call it a dirty chai, some call it a speeder chai, but at Earwax Cafe in Chicago, we called it a Bike Messenger Chai. If you saw a guy (or girl) walk in with one rolled-up pant leg, a little cap and some weirdly placed tattoos, that was a sign to pull a few shots and start steaming some chai. These barista-inspired brownies are dark and chocolaty with a spicy chai glaze.

Makes 9 big brownies

Ingredients

BROWNIES:

⅓ cup (77 g) pureed tofu

¼ cup (60 ml) brewed espresso or very strong coffee

½ cup (118 ml) canola oil

½ teaspoon almond extract

1 cup (125 g) all-purpose flour

1 cup (125 g) confectioners' sugar

½ cup (59 g) unsweetened cocoa powder

1 tablespoon (9 g) cornstarch

½ teaspoon baking powder

½ teaspoon salt

¾ cup (128 g) vegan chocolate chips

CHAI GLAZE:

1 tablespoon (14 g) vegan margarine, melted

1 tablespoon (15 ml) brewed black tea

½ teaspoon vanilla extract

¼ teaspoon ground cinnamon

¼ teaspoon ground cloves

¼ teaspoon ground ginger

¼ teaspoon ground cardamom

¾ cup (94 g) confectioners' sugar

Directions

Preheat your oven to 325°F (170°C) and line a 9 x 9-inch (23 x 23 cm) pan with parchment paper.

To make the brownies: In a small bowl, whisk together the tofu, espresso, oil and almond extract. In a large bowl, sift together the flour, sugar, cocoa powder, cornstarch, baking powder and salt. Stir the wet ingredients into the dry until well combined. Stir in the chocolate chips. Spread batter in the lined pan and bake for 20 to 25 minutes, until the edges are firm and a toothpick inserted into the center comes out with some crumbs attached. Let cool in the pan on a wire rack for at least an hour.

To make the glaze, stir all the ingredients together with a fork, adding more tea if it seems thick. Transfer the glaze into a resealable plastic bag. Squeeze out the air, then seal the bag. Snip off a tip and drizzle the glaze over the cooled brownies. Allow the glaze to set up about for 15 minutes before cutting and serving.

Party Tip: This recipe makes a cake-like brownie. For a chewier, fudgier brownie recipe, check out Black Metal Forest Brownies on page 41!

Black Metal Forest Brownies

The Black Forest is a gorgeous mountain range in Baden-Württemberg, Germany. The Black Metal Forest is a fictional place in Norway where Fenriz from Darkthrone and I bake brownies and slice them with battle-axes. I've adapted a formerly top-secret fudgy brownie recipe from my friend Melissa Elliott, author of *The Vegan Girl's Guide to Life,* to create this cherry-infused true metal confection.

Makes 9 big brownies

Ingredients

2 cups (250 g) all-purpose flour

⅔ cup (79 g) unsweetened cocoa powder

¾ teaspoon baking powder

¾ teaspoon salt

1 tablespoon (7 g) ground flaxseeds

2 cups (400 g) sugar

½ cup (120 ml) canola oil

⅔ cup (160 ml) water

1 teaspoon vanilla extract

½ cup (85 g) vegan chocolate chips

⅓ cup (82 g) cherry pie filling

Whipped Coconut Cream (page 49)

Vegan dark chocolate shavings

Directions

Preheat your oven to 350°F (180°C). Line a 9 x 9-inch (23 x 23 cm) pan with parchment paper or grease lightly.

Sift the flour, cocoa powder, baking powder and salt together in a small bowl. Stir in the ground flaxseeds. In a large bowl, whisk together the sugar, oil, water and vanilla. Stir the dry ingredients into the wet; the batter will be thick. Fold in the chocolate chips and scoop into the prepared pan. Drop the cherry pie filling by the tablespoonful on top of the batter and use a knife to swirl it in.

Bake until the sides are set up—the middle will look kind of wet and crackled—about 35 minutes.

Before serving, top each cooled brownie with a swirl of Whipped Coconut Cream and dark chocolate shavings.

German's Chocolate Cookies

Sprechen Sie Deutsch? Well, you don't have to, because contrary to popular belief, combining chocolate, coconut and pecans is not actually a German tradition. Rather, German chocolate is named for Sam German, who developed the extra-sweet, light chocolate flavor. Take that, everything you ever believed in! These lightly chocolate, chewy treats give you the German chocolate cake experience to-go!

Makes about 30 cookies

Ingredients

1 ⅔ cups (207 g) all-purpose flour

⅓ cup (40 g) white whole wheat flour

⅓ cup (39 g) unsweetened cocoa powder

½ teaspoon baking soda

½ teaspoon baking powder

¾ teaspoon salt

1 ½ cups (300 g) sugar

⅔ cup (160 ml) soy milk

⅔ cup (160 ml) canola oil

2 tablespoons (14 g) ground flaxseeds

1 teaspoon vanilla extract

1 ⅓ cups (120 g) old-fashioned rolled oats

¾ cup (128 g) vegan chocolate chips

½ cup (46 g) shredded coconut

½ cup (55 g) chopped pecans

Directions

Preheat your oven to 350°F (180°C). Line baking sheets with parchment paper.

In a large bowl, sift together the flours, cocoa powder, baking soda, baking powder and salt. In a medium bowl, whisk together the sugar, soy milk, oil, flaxseeds and vanilla. Whisk for about 2 minutes, until the mixture thickens. Stir the wet ingredients into the flour mixture until just mixed. Fold in the oats, chocolate chips, coconut and pecans.

Drop by the heaping tablespoon (18 ml) onto the prepared baking sheets and bake for 10 to 12 minutes, until the edges are set up. Let cool on the pans for 5 minutes, then let cool completely on wire racks.

Party Tip: Because it doesn't contain any eggs, a little undercooked cookie dough won't make you sick, so I like to slightly underbake these for a chewier cookie.

Fruit Punch Winkies

There's an awesome vegan bakery in Ohio called Bombshell Bake Shop. It makes some of the best cookies I've ever had, but of all its creations, my favorite is the Fruit Punch Vinkie, a fruity, vegan version of a certain oblong snack cake you all know and love. Get it? V(egan)(Tw)inkie? If you find yourself in the Buckeye State, make sure you get your hands on one, but until then, take comfort in my version—the Winkie—wink, wink!

Makes about 16

Ingredients

CAKES:

1 (0.16-ounce [4.5 g]) envelope Tropical Punch Kool-Aid

1 batch DIY Vanilla Cake Mix, prepared as a batter (page 33)

FILLING:

¼ cup (57 g) unhydrogenated vegetable shortening

¼ cup (57 g) vegan margarine

1 ¾ cups (219 g) confectioners' sugar

2 to 3 tablespoons (30 to 45 ml) soy milk

1 ¼ teaspoons vanilla extract

¼ teaspoon coconut flavoring

Pinch of salt

Directions

Preheat your oven to 350°F (180°C). Grease canoe pans or prepare homemade pans as described on page 181.

Stir the Kool-Aid into the cake batter. Scoop ¼ cup (60 ml) of batter into each cavity of the prepared pan. Bake for 18 to 20 minutes, until the tops of the cakes spring back when lightly touched. Let cool in the pans for 5 minutes, then turn out the cakes onto a wire rack and let cool completely.

While the cakes cool, make the filling: Beat together the shortening and margarine until well combined. Add the sugar and beat for 3 minutes. Add 2 tablespoons (30 ml) of soy milk and the vanilla and coconut flavoring and beat until fluffy—about 5 minutes. If the filling consistency is too thick, add up to another tablespoon (15 ml) of soy milk.

If your canoe pan came with a frosting syringe, just load it up and inject each cake with three shots of filing—inject on the flat side, which is the bottom. Otherwise, attach a pastry tip with a narrow end into a resealable plastic bag or pastry bag, fill the bag with icing and use the tip to inject the icing into each cake.

Cujo Chow

Rabid Puppy Chow fans might recognize some of these ingredients. (Heh, get it? *Rabid*.) "Puppy Chow," for the rest of you, is the somewhat unappetizing name for the traditional mix of chocolate, peanut butter, and rice cereal that showed up most often at sleepovers and school parties. In this version I've added some tasty new elements and even a superfood or two for good measure.

Serves 12 to 14

Ingredients

9 cups (279 g) Corn or Rice Chex cereal
1 cup (146 g) salted cashews
1 cup (93 g) shredded coconut
½ cup (75 g) raisins
1 ¼ cups (214 g) vegan chocolate chips
¾ cup (195 g) peanut butter
¼ cup (57 g) vegan margarine
1 teaspoon vanilla extract
¼ cup (28 g) flaxseeds
1 ½ cups (187 g) confectioners' sugar

Directions

Place the cereal, cashews, coconut and raisins in a large bowl and set aside. Place the chocolate chips, peanut butter and margarine in a microwave-safe bowl and microwave for 1 minute. Stir, then microwave for another 30 seconds if everything hasn't melted yet. Stir in the vanilla and pour over the top of the cereal mixture. Mix everything together, then sprinkle with the flaxseeds and stir those in.

Place the mixture inside a 2-gallon (7.6 L) resealable plastic bag, add the confectioners' sugar and close the top. Shake until everything is coated. Spread on waxed paper to let cool.

Caramel Sauce

This is an all-purpose caramel sauce—drizzle it on top of nondairy ice cream, use it to fill cakes and cupcakes or take shots of it as part of the world's coolest drinking game. Just as butter is the star of the show in conventional caramel, margarine is center stage in this recipe, so make sure you use a buttery, tasty margarine.

Makes about 2 cups (475 ml)

Ingredients

2 tablespoons (16 g) arrowroot starch
¾ cup (175 ml) plain soy milk
½ cup (113 g) vegan margarine
⅓ cup (105 g) pure maple syrup
1 cup (200 g) sugar
½ teaspoon salt
1 teaspoon vanilla extract

Directions

In a large measuring cup, whisk the arrowroot starch into the soy milk and set aside.

In a large saucepan over medium-low heat, cook the margarine, maple syrup, sugar and salt. Stirring constantly, cook until the margarine melts and the mixture begins to bubble.

Add the soy milk mixture and turn up the heat to medium. Cook, whisking often, until the mixture bubbles again. Remove from the heat and stir in the vanilla.

Let cool in the pan for 15 minutes, then transfer to your preferred storage container. Refrigerate for up to 2 weeks.

Party Tip: If you're a coconut fan, substitute a coconut spread for the margarine in this recipe, as I did for the Samoa Joe Cupcake recipe (page 17). Play with different flavor extracts, such as citrus or hot cinnamon, to make a variety of tasty sauces!

Whipped Coconut Cream

This recipe pops up a lot in this book because it's the easiest, healthiest way I've found to make a vegan whipped cream. No expensive stabilizers or magic tricks required. Add ¼ to ½ teaspoon of your favorite flavor extract, or add a pinch of espresso powder, ground cinnamon or cocoa powder for bazillions of different flavored whipped creams.

Makes enough for one 9 x 13-inch (23 x 33 cm) cake or 12 cupcakes

Ingredients

3 (13.3-ounce [403 ml]) cans full-fat coconut milk (see note)

½ cup (62 g) confectioners' sugar

Directions

Place the coconut milk and whisk attachment for your mixer in the refrigerator. Chill for 4 to 12 hours, I leave them overnight.

Without shaking them, open the cans of coconut milk and scoop out the thick cream on top—you should get close to ½ cup (10 ml) from each can. Place the cream in your mixing bowl, add the sugar and beat with the chilled whisk for 1 to 2 minutes, until it's thick and fluffy.

Note: I like Aroy-D, which can be found in Asian markets, but any full-fat coconut milk in a can should do the trick. Check the ethnic aisle at your grocery store!

Party Tip: Whipped Coconut Cream sets up when chilled, so you can refrigerate it for about 30 minutes, then scoop it into a piping bag if you want to be fancy. If you refrigerate frosted cakes, be sure to let them sit out for about a half hour before serving so the whipped cream softens.

The Deserker: Ideas for Making Your Desserts Completely Ridiculous

Not too long ago, I received what has come to be known as the Greatest E-mail Ever. It was from my friend James (holler at him on Twitter at @chillhartman) and it contained his detailed plans for creating the ultimate dessert—a dessert so sweet and decadent, so over the top, it could only be called The Deserker. The plans called for stuffing a cake with a pie, which is first stuffed with cookies. This idea, which we have yet to execute due to structural concerns and also not wanting to die of a heart attack, has inspired these suggestions for taking your desserts up a notch on the ladder of ridiculousness.

LADDER OF RIDICULOUSNESS

Beyond the Permafrost

You know what's awesome? Frosting. You know what's more awesome? Frosting with delicious stuff crushed up inside of it. Use your food processor to crush up cookies and/or candy and add anywhere from ¼ to ½ cup (55 to 115 g) to your favorite frosting as you whip it up. Here are some of my favorite vegan additions:

- Chick-O-Sticks
- Vegan chocolate sandwich cookies
- Vegan pretzels
- Potato chips

- Spicy hard candies, such as Brach's Cinnamon Hard Candy or Atomic Fireballs
- Nutter Butter cookies
- Lemonheads

Do the Cake Shake

Childhood birthday parties were torture—party dresses, frilly socks, someone else's mom bossing me around—but there was one thing that got me through it: mashing my cake and ice cream together and enjoying the taste sensation that occurs when the two collide. The formula is simple, you blend one piece of frosted cake with a couple scoops of nondairy ice cream, and drink it up with the fattest straw you can find. It's the perfect send-off for the last, kinda stale slice of birthday cake. Or you can whip one up from scratch, as I did with my TLC Cake Crew Challenge–winning recipe, Cake Shake, Rattle and Roll. You can check out my how-to video on my blog!

Madame Cookiebottom

Give your cupcakes a little extra something by dropping your favorite vegan chocolate sandwich cookie into the bottom of each paper liner before you add the batter. The cookie will soften once it's baked, giving each bite a boost of chocolate and frosting. It's also a fast and easy way to make two-bite cheesecakes—just toss a cookie in the bottom, top with cheesecake batter and bake. I've tried this with lots of other 2-inch (5 cm) cookies and although I certainly didn't kick any of them out of bed, sandwich cookies remain my favorite Cookiebottom component.

Chapter 2

Morning Munchies

As you read through my breakfast recipes you might start noticing a recurring theme: my trying my best to outsmart my cranky, stupid, morning self. I know most people moan and groan about getting out of bed in the morning, but I don't know many who literally hiss at the breaking dawn. I am that person. I spend my first several minutes of wakefulness trying to think of reasons to stay in bed. *Does my throat feel funny? I think my throat feels funny. If I get out of bed everyone else will get sick too. It's best that I just stay here.*

The one thing that does eventually force me to shuffle out of the bedroom is the fact that I am starving. Becoming an adult and graduating to healthy foods ruined cold cereal for me, and oatmeal just looks like depression in a bowl. Cold pizza will do in a pinch, but why not live a little?

In this chapter you'll find a versatile breakfast cookie for your first meal on the go, French toast inspired by an Elvis-impersonating pro-wrestler, whole wheat donuts, two-toned muffins and a green smoothie disguised as a milk shake.

With a little planning—sometimes as little as making sure you have flour and maple syrup—you, too, can make vegan breakfasts worth getting out of bed for. In fact, you might even find yourself tossing together a tofu scramble for dinner or snacking on a healthy donut at midday. I bet you will.

Honky Tonk French Toast

Traditionally in the baking world, the combo of peanut butter and banana calls for naming your dish after Elvis Presley, who loved peanut butter and banana sandwiches almost as much as he loved prescription drugs and rhinestones. But what I've done here is put the peanut butter and banana into the bread, then soaked it in peanut butter custard, making it an Elvis-inspired ass kicker much like professional wrestler Honky Tonk Man. Make the bread the night before you want to make French toast, to give it time to dry out properly.

Serves 6 to 8

Ingredients

BANANA BREAD:

1 ¾ cups (219 g) all-purpose flour

2 teaspoons baking powder

¼ teaspoon baking soda

¼ teaspoon ground allspice

½ teaspoon salt

⅓ cup (76 g) unhydrogenated vegetable shortening

¾ cup (195 g) crunchy or smooth natural peanut butter

⅔ cup (134 g) sugar

3 large, mashed bananas

½ teaspoon vanilla extract

FRENCH TOAST IT WITH:

1 cup (260 g) smooth peanut butter

1 ½ cups (355 ml) soy milk

2 tablespoons (19 g) cornstarch or (16 g) arrowroot starch

1 teaspoon vanilla extract

1 teaspoon ground cinnamon

1 tablespoon (15 ml) oil, for pan

Directions

Preheat your oven to 350°F (180°C). Grease and flour a 9 x 5-inch (23 x 7.5 cm) loaf pan.

To make the banana bread: In a small bowl, sift together the flour, baking powder, baking soda, allspice and salt. In a medium-size bowl, cream the shortening and peanut butter, then beat in the sugar, bananas and vanilla. With a wooden spoon, stir the dry ingredients into the wet. Pour the batter into the prepared loaf pan and bake for 40 to 50 minutes, until golden brown and a knife inserted into the middle comes out clean. Let cool in the pan for 15 minutes, then remove from the pan and let cool completely on a wire rack.

When completely cool, cut the bread into slices and store uncovered until the slices are no longer soft. (Overnight should work.)

Make the French toast: Preheat your oven to 350°F (180°C). Place the peanut butter in a microwave-safe bowl and zap it for 30 to 60 seconds, until it's melted. Whisk the melted peanut butter with the soy milk, cornstarch, vanilla and cinnamon. Lay out slices of banana bread on a rimmed baking sheet and pour the peanut butter mixture over the top, then flip the slices to coat them. Soak for about 10 minutes.

Place the soaked banana bread slices on a lightly greased baking sheet and bake for 30 minutes, turning over once halfway through. French toast has been achieved once the slices are warm and slightly crispy.

Serve warm with maple syrup and slices of fresh banana.

You Don't Know Jack Hash

As you now know, I wake up mega-grumpy and tired, so I like to prep breakfast the night before so I have a reason to get out of bed in the morning. Cook your jackfruit and chop your sweet potatoes before you go to sleep and wake up to a smoky sweet hash that will knock that crabby look off your face.

Serves 4 to 6

Ingredients

SMOKY JACKFRUIT:

1 (20-ounce [567 g]) can young jackfruit in brine

1 tablespoon (15 ml) olive oil

2 cloves minced garlic

½ cup (125 g) tomato puree

¼ cup (60 ml) water

1 tablespoon (4 g) nutritional yeast

1 tablespoon (15 ml) Bragg Liquid Aminos or soy sauce

1 tablespoon (20 g) pure maple syrup

1 teaspoon onion powder

1 teaspoon hickory liquid smoke

1 teaspoon smoked paprika

½ teaspoon salt

HASH:

4 cups (720 g) peeled and diced sweet potatoes (about 2 potatoes)

1 tablespoon (15 ml) olive oil

1 medium-size onion, diced

1 cup (120 g) chopped, toasted walnuts

Directions

Make the smoky jackfruit: Drain and wash the jackfruit, then squeeze out as much of the water as you can. Heat the oil in a medium-size skillet over a medium flame, sauté the garlic for 1 minute, then add the jackfruit and cook for 3 to 4 minutes.

Meanwhile, in a large bowl, mix together the tomato puree, water, nutritional yeast, Bragg, maple syrup, onion powder, liquid smoke, paprika and salt. Stir the cooked jackfruit into the tomato mixture and transfer to a slow cooker.

Cook on high, stirring every 15 minutes or so and adding water as needed. When the jackfruit is tender, after about 1 hour, remove from the slow cooker and use two forks to shred it. Transfer to a covered container and refrigerate for several hours or overnight.

Make the hash: Place the sweet potatoes in a large microwave-safe bowl with ½ cup (120 ml) of water. Cover and microwave on high until the potatoes are tender, 8 to 10 minutes, drain and set aside.

Add the oil to a large skillet and heat over medium-high heat. Sauté the onion until soft and translucent, 6 to 8 minutes, then add the sweet potatoes, walnuts and jackfruit. Cook until the potatoes begin to brown, 5 to 8 minutes. If needed, add a splash more oil to finish cooking.

The Early Bird Special

I came up with this recipe one cold Chicago winter morning as I was missing my grandparents' sunny retirement village in Florida. The best thing about summers with Don and Sharon is going out for a late breakfast. I walk away so full of pancakes. I'm not hungry until dinner at four in the afternoon. I translated pancake breakfast flavors into donuts because you can't dunk pancakes into coffee! Serve this maple-cinnamon donut with Orange Juice Granita (page 82) and eat while watching the Weather Channel at top volume.

Makes 12 donuts

Ingredients

2 cups (250 g) all-purpose flour

2 teaspoons baking powder

1 teaspoon salt

1 teaspoon ground cinnamon

½ teaspoon ground nutmeg

½ cup (75 g) brown sugar

¼ cup (79 g) pure maple syrup

1 tablespoon (14 g) vegan margarine, melted and cooled

1 very ripe banana, mashed

¾ cup (175 ml) soy milk

½ teaspoon vanilla extract

½ teaspoon maple flavoring

1 (5-ounce [140 g]) package of your favorite veggie bacon (see note)

2 tablespoons (30 ml) oil

Directions

Preheat your oven to 325°F (170°C) and grease your donut pan.

In a large bowl, mix together the flour, baking powder, salt, cinnamon and nutmeg. Set aside. In a small bowl, mix together the brown sugar, maple syrup, margarine, banana, soy milk, vanilla and maple flavoring. Stir the wet ingredients into the dry, mixing just until combined.

Fill each donut cavity two-thirds full and bake for 10 to 12 minutes, or until the tops spring back when lightly touched. Remove from the pans while still hot and let cool on a wire rack.

While the donuts are baking, start cooking your bacon, if using. Using a pizza cutter, cut each slice of cold veggie bacon into four thin strips. Heat the oil in a large skillet. Carefully drop the strips into the hot oil, and use a pair of tongs to shape the cooking bacon into a pile or "nest." Place the nest atop the warm donuts and drizzle with maple syrup.

Note: If you're skipping the veggie bacon, I recommend tossing ½ cup (60 g) of chopped, toasted walnuts or pecans into the batter to give this soft donut some crunch.

Whole Wheat Choco-Coconut Donuts

This isn't your typical chocolate donut. Made with whole wheat flour and tofu, this donut could serve as an actual breakfast, not some shameful thing you grab on your way to work. It's fluffy and light, almost like German chocolate cake. For an even more indulgent donut, add ½ cup (86 g) of chopped dark chocolate and ½ cup (55 g) of pecans to the batter.

Makes 12 donuts

Ingredients

2 cups (240 g) whole wheat pastry flour

¼ cup (29 g) unsweetened cocoa powder

1 teaspoon baking powder

½ teaspoon baking soda

½ teaspoon salt

2 tablespoons (30 ml) canola oil

¼ cup (60 g) pureed tofu or vegan soy yogurt

½ cup (75 g) brown sugar

¾ cup (175 ml) coconut milk

½ cup (120 ml) soy milk

1 cup (93 g) shredded coconut

OPTIONAL CHOCOLATE GLAZE:

1 cup (170 g) chopped vegan chocolate or chocolate chips

Directions

Preheat your oven to 350°F (180°C). Grease your donut pan.

In a large bowl, sift together the flour, cocoa powder, baking powder, baking soda and salt. In a medium-size bowl, whisk together the oil, tofu, brown sugar, coconut milk and soy milk. Stir the coconut mixture into the flour mixture just until incorporated. Fold in the shredded coconut and fill the donut cavities half-full. Bake for 12 to 15 minutes, or until the tops spring back when lightly touched. Let cool in the pan for 5 minutes, then transfer to a wire rack to cool completely.

To make the optional chocolate glaze: Place about 2 inches (5 cm) of water in a large pot and place over medium heat. Place the chocolate into a large, heatproof bowl and place the bowl over the pot of hot water. Stir as the chocolate melts, then remove from the heat. Dip each donut into the chocolate and set on waxed paper. Let rest until the chocolate sets, about 10 minutes.

Banana Carrot Cake Donuts

I was, and still am, the weird kid who preferred carrot cake to chocolate. The shredded texture, unexpected sweetness, and all the spices that go along with it make carrot cake something special. Celebrate your inner weird kid with these tasty donuts featuring a tropical coconut and pineapple glaze.

Makes 12 donuts

Ingredients

DONUTS:

½ cup (113 g) vegan margarine

⅔ cup (100 g) brown sugar

½ teaspoon salt

½ teaspoon vanilla extract

1 ripe banana, mashed

¼ cup (60 ml) soy milk

⅔ cup (73 g) finely shredded carrots

¾ cup (90 g) chopped walnuts

2 cups (250 g) all-purpose flour

2 teaspoons ground cinnamon

½ teaspoon ground nutmeg

1 ½ teaspoons baking powder

1 ½ teaspoons baking soda

PINEAPPLE COCONUT GLAZE:

¼ cup (60 ml) cream of coconut

¼ cup (40 g) chopped fresh pineapple

3 cups (375 g) confectioners' sugar

2 to 3 tablespoons (30 to 45 ml) soy milk

Directions

Preheat your oven to 325°F (170°C). Spray your donut pan with nonstick cooking spray.

For the donuts, cream together the margarine, brown sugar and salt in a large bowl. Add the banana, soy milk and vanilla and beat until smooth. Stir in the carrots and walnuts.

In a large bowl, sift together the flour, cinnamon, nutmeg, baking powder and baking soda. Slowly add the dry ingredients to the wet, stirring until combined.

Fill the donut cavities half-full. Bake for 12 to 15 minutes. Let cool in the pan for 5 minutes before transferring to a wire rack to cool completely.

For the glaze, toss the cream of coconut, pineapple and confectioners' sugar in a food processor and pulse until smooth. Add soy milk as needed to achieve a dunkable texture. Dip each donut into the glaze and set on waxed paper or a wire rack. Let rest until the glaze sets up, about 5 minutes.

Breakfast Bites

If you're like me in the morning, you can't be bothered with preparing a proper first meal. Make these wholesome oatmeal bites the night before and cut back on grouchiness by 75 percent. (This statement has not been evaluated by the FDA and is most likely made up.) They're yummy and chewy as is, or you can smear them with almond butter or toss them into your favorite nondairy yogurt for an instant parfait. Feel free to swap in your favorite dried fruit and nuts.

Makes about 30 cookies

Ingredients

1 very ripe banana, mashed

¼ cup (60 g) all-natural applesauce

2 tablespoons (30 ml) canola oil

2 tablespoons (40 g) pure maple syrup or agave nectar

Juice from ½ lemon

1 teaspoon vanilla extract

1 cup (80 g) old-fashioned rolled oats

½ cup (60 g) whole wheat pastry flour

½ cup (46 g) coconut flakes

½ cup (60 g) chopped walnuts

⅓ cup (80 g) dried cranberries

2 tablespoons (14 g) ground flaxseeds

1 tablespoon (6 g) peeled and diced fresh ginger, or more or less to taste

Zest of 1 organic lemon

½ teaspoon salt

½ teaspoon ground cinnamon

Directions

Preheat your oven to 350°F (180°C) and line two baking sheets with parchment paper or silicone mats.

In a small bowl, combine the banana, applesauce, oil, maple syrup, lemon juice and vanilla. In a large bowl, combine the oats, flour, coconut, walnuts, cranberries, flaxseeds, ginger, lemon zest, salt and cinnamon. Pour the wet ingredients into the dry, and stir to mix. Scoop a heaping tablespoon (20 g) of dough onto the baking sheet, leaving at least 1 inch (2.5 cm) between each cookie. Use your palm to slightly flatten the tops. Bake for 20 to 22 minutes, until the tops and edges are lightly browned. Transfer the cookies to a wire rack to cool completely.

The Non-Cop-out Tofu Scramble

According to my friend Ricky, tofu scramble is the ultimate vegan cop-out. It's hard to argue otherwise—often beige and flavorless, it's the staple vegan item on most contemporary diners' menus. With this Greek-inspired recipe, I set out not just to reclaim tofu scramble, but also to shove it in Ricky's face. Earthy Italian seasoning collides with tart lemon juice and kalamata olives, making this scramble anything but a cop-out; rather, a savory delight.

Serves 4 to 6

Ingredients

2 tablespoons (30 ml) oil

4 cloves garlic, minced

1 (14-ounce [397 g]) block extra-firm tofu, drained

1 tablespoon (4 g) Italian seasoning

½ teaspoon salt

3 tablespoons (45 ml) freshly squeezed lemon juice

¼ cup (16 g) nutritional yeast

¼ cup (39 g) sun-dried tomatoes, chopped

⅓ cup (55 g) kalamata olives, sliced

A few handfuls of spinach, washed and chopped

Directions

Heat the oil in a large skillet over medium-high heat and cook the minced garlic for about 1 minute, stirring often. Break the tofu into bite-size pieces and add it to the pan. Cook for about 10 minutes, using a metal spatula to turn the tofu over and to scrape the bottom of the pan now and again.

In a small bowl or mixing cup, stir together the Italian seasoning, salt and lemon juice. Add this mixture and the nutritional yeast to the tofu and cook for 5 more minutes. Add the tomatoes, olives and spinach and cook just until the spinach wilts, 2 to 3 minutes.

Mighty Migas

My sister asked me to write this recipe for her husband, Will. He looks exactly like pro-wrestler Ricky "the Dragon" Steamboat, so I will basically do anything for him. Migas is an egg dish popular in the Southwest. It uses up leftover tortillas to make a stick-to-your ribs breakfast fit for a Texan. I've used tofu in place of eggs here, and replaced chorizo with black beans, but otherwise stayed true to the original recipe to make Will "the Steamboat" happy.

Serves 4 to 6

Ingredients

2 tablespoons (30 ml) oil

1 (14-ounce [397 g]) block extra-firm tofu, drained

½ sweet onion, chopped

1 cup (70 g) sliced mushrooms

½ red bell pepper, seeded and chopped

1 chipotle chile in adobo sauce, rinsed and finely chopped

1 (15-ounce [425 g]) can black beans, drained and rinsed

1 ripe tomato, diced

¼ cup (16 g) nutritional yeast

½ teaspoon salt, plus more to taste

8 ounces (225 g) spinach leaves, chopped

Freshly ground black pepper

1 tablespoon (15 ml) vegetable oil

4 to 6 corn tortillas (see Party Tip)

OPTIONAL

Chopped fresh cilantro

Peeled, pitted and diced avocado

1 lime, cut into wedges

Directions

Heat the 2 tablespoons (30 ml) of oil in a large skillet over medium-high heat. Break the tofu into bite-size pieces and add it to the pan. Cook for 5 minutes, using a metal spatula to turn the tofu over occasionally. Throw in the onion, mushrooms, red bell pepper and chipotle chile. Cook for 5 more minutes. Add the black beans, tomatoes, nutritional yeast and ½ teaspoon of salt and cook 5 more minutes. Migas is traditionally a moist dish, but if after 5 minutes it looks too wet for your taste, turn up the heat and cook off some of the excess moisture.

While that cooks, fry the tortillas: Heat the 1 tablespoon (15 ml) of oil in a heavy skillet and fry the tortillas one at a time, until they start to brown, making sure to flip them and cook both sides. Stack the cooked tortillas on a cutting board and use a sharp knife to chop into bite-size pieces.

Add the spinach to the tofu, and cook just until it begins to wilt, 2 to 3 minutes. Remove from the heat and stir in the tortilla pieces just before serving. Add salt and pepper to taste. Serve topped with cilantro, and chunks of avocado and lime, if desired.

Party Tip: If you don't normally have corn tortillas lying around the house—*what is wrong with you?* Anyway, if that's not your thing, you can smash up some tortilla chips and use them instead.

This Granola Bar Will Save Your Life

Back before people could just Google themselves out of terrible situations, I found myself hungry and lost in Toledo, Ohio. A greasy diner was the only source of food for miles and not even the hamburger buns were vegan. If only I'd had these granola bars in my pocket I might not have eaten ketchup for dinner that night. Save yourself. Carry these sweet-and-spicy granola bars with you always.

Makes 14 to 16 bars

Ingredients

2 cups (160 g) old-fashioned rolled oats

¾ cup (105 g) wheat germ

¾ cup (109 g) sunflower seeds

½ cup (65 g) almond slivers

½ cup (71 g) cashews, crushed

1 tablespoon (6 g) peeled and minced fresh ginger

1 cup (120 g) dried cranberries

⅔ cup (100 g) brown sugar

½ cup (162 g) agave nectar

¼ cup (57 g) vegan margarine

1 teaspoon ground cinnamon

½ teaspoon ground cardamom

¼ teaspoon ground cloves

½ teaspoon salt

2 teaspoons vanilla extract

Directions

Preheat your oven to 400°F (200°C).

On a baking sheet with raised sides, stir together the oats, wheat germ, sunflower seeds, almonds and cashews. Bake for 8 to 10 minutes, stirring often, until toasted. Remove from the oven, transfer to a large bowl and stir in the ginger and cranberries.

Line a 11 x 13-inch (28 x 33 cm) baking dish with parchment paper and spray with nonstick spray. (A smaller pan, such as a 9 x 13-inch [23 x 33 cm], is fine, it will just result in thicker bars.)

In a saucepan over medium heat, bring the brown sugar, agave, margarine, cinnamon, cardamom, cloves and salt to a simmer, stirring constantly. Remove from the heat and stir in the vanilla. Pour this mixture over the nut mixture and stir so everything is coated. Transfer to the prepared baking dish and use a rubber spatula to spread out the mixture and press it into the pan.

Place a sheet of waxed paper on top and press down hard to compact the mixture into the pan. Let this cool in the pan for 2 to 3 hours, then turn out onto a cutting board and use a large knife to cut into bars.

Preheat your oven to 300°F (150°C), and place the cut bars on a baking sheet lined with parchment paper. Bake for 20 minutes, or until the edges start to brown. Let cool completely, then store in an airtight container or plastic wrap.

Chai Berry Muffins

I have earned a reputation, at least with my husband, for being a spice addict. He sees "cardamom-rosewater" or "clove-infused" on a menu and shoots a knowing glance my way. I love spicy spices and I don't care who knows. Haters will try to tell you that spice muffins are just for cold weather, so I stuffed these spicy muffins with juicy summer berries. Try and hate on that, sucka.

Makes 12 muffins

Ingredients

¾ cup (175 ml) soy or rice milk

2 black tea bags

1 ¾ cups (219 g) all-purpose flour

⅔ cup (134 g) sugar

1 tablespoon (14 g) baking powder

2 teaspoons ground cinnamon

1 teaspoon ground cardamom

½ teaspoon ground ginger

¼ teaspoon ground cloves

½ teaspoon salt

Pinch of ground white pepper

1 cup (150 g) frozen mixed berries

2 ½ tablespoons (17 g) ground flaxseeds

3 tablespoons (45 ml) water

⅓ cup (80 ml) canola or vegetable oil

Directions

Preheat your oven to 400°F (200°C). Grease a twelve-cup muffin pan.

Heat the soy milk on the stovetop or in a microwave until almost boiling, add the tea bags and steep for 3 to 4 minutes. Remove the tea bags and let cool. In a large bowl, whisk together the flour, sugar, baking powder, cinnamon, cardamom, ginger, cloves, salt and pepper. Stir in the frozen berries. In a small bowl, whisk the ground flaxseeds and water together. Add this, the tea mixture and the oil to the dry flour mixture. Stir just until mixed; the batter will be lumpy. Scoop the batter into the muffin pan and bake for 20 to 25 minutes, or until a toothpick inserted into the center comes out clean. Let cool for 1 minute before removing from the pan.

Breakfast Pizza

This dish is one of my husband's many contributions to this book. (He made me say that.)
If, like us, you believe that a hearty Sunday morning breakfast should be followed immediately by
a nap, you will appreciate the genius of a tender biscuit crust topped with savory gravy and tender tofu
scramble. For convenience's sake, you can prepare the gravy and tofu one day ahead of time,
and just make the crust fresh in the morning.

Serves 6 to 8

Ingredients

GRAVY:

2 tablespoons (28 g) vegan margarine

2 teaspoons soy sauce or Bragg Liquid Aminos

¼ cup (31 g) all-purpose flour

1 cup (235 ml) vegetable broth

1 cup (235 ml) plain soy milk

½ teaspoon onion powder

½ teaspoon garlic powder

2 tablespoons (8 g) nutritional yeast

1 tablespoon (2.5 g) chopped fresh sage

½ teaspoon apple cider vinegar

Salt and freshly ground black pepper

TOFU SCRAMBLE:

2 tablespoons (30 ml) oil

2 cloves garlic, minced

1 (14-ounce [397 g]) block extra-firm tofu, drained

1 cup (71 g) thinly sliced broccoli

½ cup (55 g) grated carrot

1 teaspoon dried rosemary

1 teaspoon onion powder

½ teaspoon ground turmeric

½ teaspoon salt

3 tablespoons (45 ml) water

¼ cup (16 g) nutritional yeast

CRUST:

1 cup (235 ml) plain soy milk

1 teaspoon apple cider vinegar

2 cups (250 g) all-purpose flour, plus more for dusting
the board

¼ teaspoon baking soda

1 tablespoon (14 g) baking powder

1 teaspoon salt

6 tablespoons (85 g) unhydrogenated vegetable shortening

Directions

Make the gravy: In a large saucepan, melt the margarine over medium-low heat. Whisk in the soy sauce and flour and continue to whisk for 2 minutes—the mixture will form a paste. Add the vegetable broth, soy milk, onion powder, garlic powder, nutritional yeast and sage and whisk for a few minutes to break up the lumps. Raise the heat to medium-high and cook until bubbles form around the edges of the gravy, then reduce the heat to medium-low and cook until thickened, about 5 minutes. Remove from the heat and stir in the apple cider vinegar and salt and pepper to taste. Set aside.

To make tofu scramble, heat the oil in a large skillet over medium-high heat, then cook the minced garlic for about 1 minute, stirring often. Break the tofu into bite-size pieces and add it to the pan along with the broccoli and carrot. Cook for about 10 minutes, using a metal spatula to turn the mixture over and to scrape the bottom of the pan now and again. The garlic and carrot will turn into brown crispy stuff—don't worry, that stuff is good!

In a small bowl or mixing cup, stir together the rosemary, onion powder, turmeric, salt and water. Add this mixture and the nutritional yeast to the tofu and cook for 5 more minutes. Set aside and prepare the crust.

For the crust, preheat your oven to 450°F (230°C). Add the apple cider vinegar to the soy milk and set aside to curdle.

Combine the dry ingredients in a bowl and use a pastry blender or two forks to cut the shortening into the flour until it resembles coarse meal.

Add the curdled soy milk and mix just until combined. The mixture should be wet, so add a splash more soy milk if it appears dry.

Turn out the dough onto a floured countertop and gently pat it out until it's about ½ inch (1.3 cm) thick. (Using a rolling pin will result in a tough biscuit!) Fold the pressed dough into its center four or five times so you have a pile, and gently pat it out into a circle that's about ½ inch (1.3 cm) thick.

Place the dough onto a baking sheet—if you want to make it more pizzalike, press down the center slightly more so the edges are raised like a crust. Bake the biscuit crust for 5 minutes, then pull it out of the oven and top it with half of the gravy and all of the tofu scramble. Place the pizza back into the oven and cook until the biscuit is cooked through—6 to 8 more minutes. Slice and serve with the remaining warm gravy on top.

Venus Chocolate-Pumpkin Muffins

Named for Venus, the feline Internet sensation with a half-black, half-orange tabby face, these muffins take a bit more effort than their single-color counterparts, but I think you'll agree they're well worth it. This recipe makes just under a traditional dozen muffins—a quirk that I hope you will find strangely endearing, just like Venus's face.

Makes 10 to 11 muffins

Ingredients

CHOCOLATE BATTER:

1 tablespoon + ¾ teaspoon (12 g) ground flaxseeds

1 ½ tablespoons (25 ml) water

½ cup (63 g) all-purpose flour

¼ cup (30 g) white whole wheat flour

3 tablespoons (22 g) unsweetened cocoa powder (see note)

1 teaspoon baking powder

¼ teaspoon baking soda

¼ teaspoon salt

¼ cup (50 g) sugar

¼ cup (43 g) vegan chocolate chips, plus more for sprinkling

½ cup (120 ml) soy milk

3 tablespoons (45 ml) vegetable oil

½ teaspoon vanilla extract

PUMPKIN BATTER:

1 tablespoon + ¾ teaspoon (12 g) ground flaxseeds

1 ½ tablespoons (25 ml) water

½ cup (63 g) all-purpose flour

¼ cup (50 g) sugar

1 teaspoon baking powder

¾ teaspoon ground cinnamon

¼ teaspoon ground nutmeg

¼ teaspoon salt

Pinch of ground ginger

2 tablespoons (30 ml) canola oil

½ cup + 2 tablespoons (140 g) canned pure pumpkin

¼ cup (60 ml) soy milk

¾ teaspoon vanilla extract

¼ cup (30 g) chopped walnuts

STREUSEL TOPPING:

¼ cup (31 g) all-purpose flour

2 tablespoons (18 g) brown sugar

2 tablespoons (28 g) vegan margarine

Pinch of ground cinnamon

Directions

Preheat your oven to 350°F (180°C) and lightly grease a twelve-cup muffin pan or line it with paper liners.

Make the chocolate batter: In a small cup, stir together the ground flaxseeds and water until thick—about 1 minute. In a large bowl, sift together the flours, cocoa powder, baking powder, baking soda, salt and sugar. Stir in the chocolate chips. Add the soy milk, oil, and vanilla plus the flaxseed mixture, and stir until just combined—do not overmix.

Then, make the pumpkin batter: In a small cup, stir together the ground flaxseeds and water until it becomes thick—about 1 minute. In a large bowl, sift together the flour, sugar, baking powder, cinnamon, nutmeg, salt and ginger. In a smaller bowl, stir together the flaxseed mixture, oil, pumpkin, soy milk and vanilla. Gently stir the wet ingredients into the dry, then fold in the walnuts. Do not overmix.

In a small bowl, use a fork to combine the ingredients for the streusel topping. It will be a crumbly mixture.

Add equal parts of each batter to each prepared muffin cup, filling each two-thirds full. Stack one flavor on top of the other, use two spoons to scoop them in side by side, or use a toothpick to swirl the flavors together. Sprinkle the tops with streusel topping and chocolate chips, and lightly pat the toppings down into the batter.

Bake for 20 to 25 minutes, or until a toothpick inserted into the center comes out clean. Let cool in the pans for 10 minutes, then transfer to a wire rack to cool completely.

Note: For an extra-dark chocolate, use half Dutch-processed cocoa powder, half regular unsweetened cocoa powder.

Breakfast Granitas: The Slurpee's Stuck-up Cousin

A granita is a semifrozen Sicilian dessert, it's also fancy people talk for a Slurpee. As a long-time advocate of dessert for breakfast, I like to serve these lightly-sweet, frosty treats alongside Honky Tonk French Toast (page 56) or the Early Bird Special (page 61).

Each recipe serves 4 to 6

Orange Juice Granita

Who needs boring OJ? This citrus-rich granita delivers vitamin C
and a slight sugar buzz with every chilly bite.

Ingredients

1 ¼ cups (295 ml) water
½ cup (100 g) sugar
Zest of 2 organic oranges
Juice of 6 oranges (12 ounces [355 ml])
Juice of 1 lemon

Directions

In a small saucepan, bring the water, sugar and orange zest to a boil. Reduce the heat and simmer until the sugar is dissolved, about 10 minutes. Mix in the orange and lemon juice, and pour into a shallow pan. A baking sheet with raised edges works well, or use a jelly-roll pan.

Cover with foil and freeze for 1 to 2 hours, until solid around edges. Scrape the mixture with a fork, mixing from the edges inward. Repeat the freezing and scraping process every 30 minutes (at least three times), until the entire mixture is flaky.

When ready to serve, scrape into serving dishes.

Arnold Palmer Granita

Named after American golfer Arnold Palmer (how's *that* for a punk rock reference?) this half-tea, half-lemonade granita is inspired by his favorite drink—the half & half.

Ingredients

1 cup (235 ml) water

¾ cup (150 g) sugar

3 cups (710 ml) double-strength black iced tea (made with 6 tea bags + 3 cups [710 ml] water)

Juice from 2 lemons (about ½ cup [120 ml])

Directions

In a small saucepan, combine the water and sugar and heat over medium heat, stirring occasionally. Cook until the mixture begins to boil, then remove from the heat and let cool completely.

Stir the mixture together with the iced tea and lemon juice and pour into a shallow pan. A baking sheet with raised edges works well, or use a jelly-roll pan.

Cover with foil and freeze for 2 hours, until solid around edges. Scrape the mixture with a fork, mixing from the edges inward. Repeat the freezing and scraping process every 30 minutes (at least three times), until the entire mixture is flaky.

When ready to serve, scrape into serving dishes.

Double Soy Latte Granita

In hot summer months there is a nonstop supply of this caffeinated granita in my freezer—we throw it in a to-go cup and enjoy it Slurpee-style.

Ingredients

VANILLA SYRUP:

1 cup (200 g) sugar

1 cup (235 ml) water

1 tablespoon (15 ml) vanilla extract

GRANITA:

1 ½ cups (355 ml) brewed espresso or really strong coffee

1 ½ cups (355 ml) soy milk

¼ cup (60 ml) vanilla syrup (see recipe above)

⅛ teaspoon ground cinnamon

Directions

To make the vanilla syrup, stir the sugar and water together in a saucepan and cook over medium-high heat, stirring constantly. Cook until the mixture begins to boil, then turn down the heat to low and simmer, stirring often, for 5 to 7 minutes, until the mixture turns a golden color. Remove from the heat and stir in the vanilla. Allow the syrup to cool before transferring it to your preferred bottle or container. Use it in this recipe, or to easily sweeten iced coffee and tea.

To make the granita, stir its ingredients together and pour into a shallow pan. A baking sheet with raised edges works well, or use a jelly-roll pan.

Cover with foil and freeze for 1 to 2 hours until solid around edges. Scrape the mixture with a fork, mixing from the edges inward. Repeat the freezing and scraping process every 30 minutes (at least three times), until the entire mixture is flaky.

When ready to serve, scrape into serving dishes.

Smoothie Operator

I was the kid who threw things off the roof just to watch them smash on the sidewalk below—a natural-born smoothie fan. There's something about putting a bunch of perfectly good food in a blender and watching it explode that just makes me happy. Here are three of my favorite smoothies to satisfy the sadist in me.

Dan's Drinkin' Kale

The older I get, the more I realize I'm turning into my dad. I love black licorice, Hawaiian shirts and pistachio ice cream. So when I saw everyone on the Internet freaking out about a "pistachio ice cream-kale shake" I had my suspicions. My dad would never drink kale anything. After trying every version I could find, though, I came up with one worthy of Dan the Man.

Makes 1 smoothie

Ingredients

2 tablespoons (20 g) chia seeds

1 cup (235 ml) almond milk, plus a splash more as needed

½ cup (71 g) raw cashews

1 cup (67 g) curly kale leaves, stems removed

½ cup (89 g) chopped pitted dates

1 teaspoon vanilla extract, or more to taste

½ teaspoon peeled and minced ginger, or more to taste

Directions

The night before: Soak the chia seeds in the almond milk in the refrigerator overnight. Soak the cashews, too, in water—those can be left out on the countertop.

In the morning (or whenever): Scoop the chia mixture (including the almond milk) and drained cashews into your blender along with the kale, dates, vanilla and ginger. Add a few ice cubes to make it frosty, and add almond milk as needed for consistency. I like lots of vanilla and ginger in mine but, hey man, do your own thing.

Party Tip: This smoothie is also tasty with a ripe banana and some shredded coconut and/or cacao nibs.

Candy Bar Smoothie

This recipe was given to me by former WWE Women's Champion Amy "Lita" Dumas, so I can guarantee it's healthy. But it is often consumed by reigning Sitting on the Couch Watching Reruns of *Cops* Champion Natalie "Naptime" Slater, so I can also guarantee it's tasty.

Makes 1 smoothie

Ingredients

1 frozen ripe banana

½ cup (46 g) unsweetened shredded coconut

2 to 3 tablespoons (32 to 48 g) almond butter

2 tablespoons (14 g) flaxseeds

2 tablespoons (19 g) raw cocoa nibs

1 teaspoon ground cinnamon

1 teaspoon vanilla extract

Almond milk

Directions

Place the banana, coconut, almond butter, flaxseeds, cocoa nibs, cinnamon and vanilla in a blender. Cover with almond milk and blend until smooth. Add more almond milk to achieve your desired consistency.

Party Tip: Amy says to add a scoop of Sun Warrior Raw Vegan Vanilla Protein Powder if you're drinking this postworkout. I am not familiar with this "working out" thing.

Yeah, It's a Green Smoothie

I've always loved the idea of green smoothies—drinking your greens so you have more time to eat cake—but I'd never made one I could stomach until Amy (yep, same Amy from the Candy Bar Smoothie recipe) gave me her basic formula. Here's my version of her nutritious drink.

Makes 2 smoothies

Ingredients

1 frozen ripe banana

1 cup (165 g) frozen pineapple chunks

½ cup packed (30 g) baby spinach

3 to 5 stalks curly kale, stems removed

1 sprig fresh mint

1 (1" [2.5 cm])-piece fresh ginger, peeled and minced

½ lemon, rind removed

Scoop of wheat grass powder (optional)

1 teaspoon spirulina powder (optional)

12 ounces (175 ml) coconut water, plus more if needed

Directions

Blend everything together until smooth—add more coconut water if it's too thick for your taste.

Party Tip: If you're new to green smoothies, start with some mellow greens, such as baby spinach, bok choy, or chard. Kale is mega-healthy, but it's not for everyone. Sweet berries also help to mask the earthy flavor of greens that some folks aren't keen on.

Chapter 3

Party Hard Entrées

Being a grown-up does not mean trading your diet of pizza and tacos in for meat loaf and side salads, but it does mean rethinking pizza and tacos to make them healthier than meat loaf could ever dream of being.

Speaking of meat loaf, opting for a meat- and dairy-free dinner shouldn't be a one-way ticket to veggie burger hell. There are lots of easy and inexpensive things you could be eating instead of fake meats from your freezer section. (I know, because I put them in this book!)

Dig into my spicy, savory Taco Lasagna or a piping hot Samosa Potpie stuffed with peas and potatoes. Pizza for Thanksgiving dinner? My Green Bean Casserole Pizza is an obvious choice. Try a generous slice of Spaghetti Cake with Grandma's Hater-Proof Sauce—straight from my grandma Sharon's kitchen!

No matter what you choose, you won't miss fake burgers or take-out pizza, not even for a second!

Taco Lasagna

In third grade I used to spend all my Scholastic money on Garfield books. It bummed my mom out, but those books taught me two important life lessons: lasagna is awesome and Mondays suck. I don't know Garfield's opinion on Taco Lasagna, but something tells me the layers of mushrooms, corn and spicy Nacho Chee-Zee Sauce would earn this dish a furry orange thumbs-up.

Serves 8

Ingredients

FILLING:

2 teaspoons oil, for pan

12 ounces (53 g) button mushrooms, stemmed and quartered

1 clove garlic, minced

½ teaspoon salt

Freshly ground black pepper

2 (15-ounce [425 g]) cans black beans, drained and rinsed

1 ½ (15-ounce [425 g]) cans corn, or 3 ¼ cups (420 g) frozen corn

Nacho Chee-Zee Sauce (page 161)

1 (10- to 12-ounce [280 to 340 g]) jar of your favorite chunky salsa

8 soft flour tortillas

TOPPING:

Sliced black olives

1 avocado, peeled, pitted and diced

Juice from 1 lime

Directions

Preheat your oven to 400°F (200°C).

Make the filling: Heat the oil in a large skillet over medium-high heat, add the mushrooms and cook, stirring often, for about 7 minutes or until browned. Add the garlic, salt and pepper to taste. Remove from the heat.

In a medium-size bowl, mix beans, corn and mushrooms with the Nacho Chee-Zee Sauce.

Pour one-third of the salsa into the bottom of a 10-inch (25.5 cm) round or 9 x 13-inch (23 x 33 cm) oven-safe dish. Top with a layer of overlapping tortillas, similar to layering in lasagna noodles.

Top with one-third of the bean mixture, then one-quarter of the remaining salsa, and another layer of overlapping tortillas.

Repeat with another third of the bean mixture and more salsa, and top with more tortillas.

Finally, add the last third of the bean mixture and half of the remaining salsa, and top with tortillas.

Pour the remaining salsa on top and bake for 30 minutes. Let cool for 10 to 15 minutes.

Toss the avocado with the lime juice, then top the baked lasagna with the avocado mixture and olives. Slice and eat!

French Fry Tacos

For some reason, we always have an odd amount of potato products left in our freezer—fourteen Tater Tots, a handful of hash browns, a quarter of a bag of oven fries. Rather than toss out these rejected spuds, we started seasoning them and dressing them up as tacos. This recipe just calls for oven fries, but you can use any potato product you have on hand.

Serves 4 to 6

Ingredients

1 (2-pound [905 g]) bag oven fries

TACO SEASONING:

1 ½ teaspoons chili powder

1 teaspoon ground cumin

1 teaspoon salt

1 teaspoon freshly ground black pepper

¼ teaspoon garlic powder

¼ teaspoon onion powder

¼ teaspoon crushed red pepper flakes

¼ teaspoon dried oregano

FILLING:

1 tablespoon (15 ml) oil

1 (15-ounce [425 g]) can black beans, drained and rinsed

1 cup (40 g) diced red onion

2 cloves garlic, diced

1 red bell pepper, seeded and diced

½ cup (75 g) corn (frozen or canned)

Salt and freshly ground black pepper

Corn tortillas

1 avocado, peeled, pitted and sliced

2 scallions, chopped

1 large tomato, seeded and diced

1 lime

Vegan Mayo (optional, page 158)

Directions

Preheat the oven according to the directions on the bag of fries.

In a small bowl, mix together all of the taco seasoning ingredients. Open the top of the oven fries bag, pour in about one-quarter of the taco seasoning mix, hold the top of the bag closed, and shake. Add the remaining seasoning gradually, shaking after each addition, until the fries are coated. Place the fries in a single layer on a baking sheet, and bake according to the package directions. (I give them a few extra minutes so they're nice and crunchy).

While those bake, prepare the filling: In a large skillet, heat the oil over medium heat. Add the beans, onion, garlic, red bell pepper and corn. Add salt and pepper to taste and cook until the onion softens and everything is warmed through, about 10 minutes.

Heat a large skillet or griddle and warm up the tortillas, flipping to warm each side. Store the warm tortillas wrapped in a clean kitchen towel until ready to serve.

To assemble the tacos, place some fries on a tortilla, then some of the bean mixture, and top with avocado, scallions, tomato and a squeeze of lime juice. I like a dollop of Vegan Mayo on each one, too!

Be My Fantasy Pizza: Tips for Epic Pizzas Plus a Recipe for Not-Parm

In Chicago, everyone heads out to Dimo's Pizza for their comfort food–inspired 'zas. But let's face it, sometimes you're too lazy, broke or naked to leave the house for pizza—and unless you're filming a porno, you're probably not going to call for delivery when you're naked. Fear not, pizza lovers. My friends at Dimo's have been kind enough to help me come up with these tips for creating your own fantasy pizzas at home.

Break It Down

First conceptualize your pizza. Think about what foods you like, what goes well together, and most important, what you'll be capable of making. For example, say you want to turn nachos into a pizza. Start out by dissecting what makes it so dang delicious. Tortilla chips, Chee-Zee Sauce, spicy baked tofu, jalapeños and olives? So those are your ingredients, go get them!

Get Stoned

Unless you have a stone pizza deck in your house (and if you do, I hate you) you'll probably need to invest in a pizza stone. You can pick one up at Target or any kitchen store for around twenty dollars and it will last virtually forever, provided you don't wash it with soap or drop it.

- For a crispy crust, always preheat your pizza stone. To do so, place it in a cold oven, and then heat your oven, with the stone inside, to the desired temperature. Placing a cold stone in a hot oven might crack the stone.

- Before placing your dough on the stone, sprinkle the stone with cornmeal so the dough doesn't stick.

- Don't slice your pizza on the stone—transfer your pie to a cutting board or serving dish first.

- Let the stone cool down before rinsing it—hot stone + cool water = cracked stone. And don't use soap! A pizza stone's job is to absorb moisture; it will also absorb soap. Wipe it clean and let it dry.

- Throwing your dough on a hot stone can be tricky, so you might also want to get a pizza paddle (a.k.a. peel) or devise some other way to get the wiggly dough onto the stone.

Throw Up

If you're feeling adventurous enough, pick up the dough, place it over your two fists (turn your hands toward each other and pretend you've got tennis balls in each hand) and start tossing so that the dough rotates and you stretch every part of it. Don't actually throw the crust into the air; just rotate it with little flicks of your hands and pull your hands away from each other upon each rotation.

If you tear a hole in your dough, don't freak—just fold one side of the tear over the rest of the dough so it overlaps ¼ inch (6 mm) or so. Press the seam out, and keep on truckin'.

Get Sauced

Red sauce is so passé. (Unless, of course, you're making a grilled Chee-Zee and tomato soup pizza!) What else could make your pizza ooey-gooey and complement the flavor of pizza perfectly, not to mention help the rest of the toppings to stick? Get creative! Use pesto, or pureed veggies (and olives) for a savory sauce. Just remember, whatever you use, you'll want to eat your pizza slice by slice and not with a spoon. So you can go crazy, but sometimes your toppings are gooey enough, and you can skip the sauce altogether.

Math Is Hard

The trickiest part about fantasy pizza is the timing. You don't throw a raw potato covered in toppings in the oven, do you? Of course not! Occasionally your wacky pizza idea will require some prep work to make everything come out just right. Here are some timing tips to get you started:

- Slice potatoes thin for quick and even cooking.

- Cut other slow-cooking veggies, such as carrots, into a smallish dice.

- Don't bake everything—some toppings, such as dressings or Chee-Zee Sauce, look much better if they are placed on the pizza after it's cooked. Place them in a squirt bottle or in a resealable plastic bag with the corner snipped off and drizzle them over your pizza for the perfect presentation.

- Don't overtop! You should be able to taste each ingredient in every bite.

Adventures in Cheese

I might get my Chicago card pulled for saying this, but you don't need cheese on every slice of pizza! If you're using plenty of moist, fresh toppings and a savory sauce, you won't miss the cheese. And if you do miss cheese, there are lots of great nondairy alternatives these days, such as Daiya and Teese vegan cheese. Try this easy replacement for Parmesan cheese:

Not-Parm

Makes about 5 ounces (140 g)

Ingredients

1 cup (120 g) walnuts
⅓ cup (21 g) nutritional yeast
½ teaspoon seasoned salt
½ teaspoon garlic powder

Directions

Place all the ingredients in a food processor and blend until it's the texture of Parmesan cheese. Flavor your Not-Parm by adding chili powder or curry powder, or what have you.

Eternal Pizza Party

If you think pizza's only for dinner, you've been missing out. Think about pizza as a meal on an edible, delicious plate. What about a warm slice of breakfast burrito pizza with tofu scramble, beans, Chee-Zee Sauce and salsa? Ever had pizza for dessert? Toss some vegan chocolate chips and vegan marshmallows on the crust to make a s'mores pizza, or maybe some sliced peaches and brown sugar to a peach cobbler pizza. The possibilities are literally endless!

Just Do It

If at first you don't succeed, eat your mistakes and try again.

I Love the Dough

Did you know that ancient cultures believed pizza held mystical healing powers? In fact, archaeologists discovered what is believed to be the world's first pizza cutter inside Julius Caesar's tomb! That may or may not be true, but pizza's versatility and deliciousness is fact, son. What would pizza be without the crust? A mess, that's what. So channel your inner Biggie Smalls, because it's time to make this super-simple dough, which results in a perfectly chewy crust. I recommend using a pizza stone and a pizza paddle when making pizza crust. For more about pizza stones, check out Be My Fantasy Pizza on page 96.

Makes two 12-inch (30 cm) pizza crusts

Ingredients

1 (2 ¼-teaspoon [9 g]) package active dry yeast
1 ½ teaspoons sugar
3 cups (375 g) all-purpose flour

1 cup (235 ml) warm water (no more than 115°F [46°C])
1 teaspoon salt
2 tablespoons (30 ml) extra-virgin olive oil, plus more for drizzling
½ cup (85 g) cornmeal

Party Tips:

- Add your favorite herbs to this basic dough to enhance your pizza creations. Add more sugar and top it with vegan chocolate, vegan marshmallows and other good stuff for an aces dessert pizza!

- To prebake or not to prebake? If you like your crust slightly chewy, don't prebake it. If you like a crispier crust, prebake the untopped dough for 3 to 4 minutes, then take it out, add the toppings and finish baking.

Directions

In a small bowl, use a fork to combine the yeast, sugar, and ½ cup (63 g) of the flour with the warm water. It might start to bubble; try not to get scared.

Use a food processor to pulse together 2 cups (250 g) of the flour, and the olive oil and salt. (You can also do the mixing in a stand mixer fitted with a dough hook, or by hand with a wooden spoon.) Gradually add the yeast mixture and mix until it forms a ball.

Turn out the dough on a lightly floured surface and knead it for about 2 minutes. Roll it into a ball and place it in a lightly oiled large bowl and drizzle with a bit of olive oil to keep it from drying out. Cover with a clean, damp towel and let it rise in a cool spot for about 2 hours, or until the dough doubles in size. I like to prep my toppings while the dough rises.

Divide the dough into two balls (heh). Knead each ball a few times—if you don't plan on making two pizzas, you can stick one ball in a resealable plastic bag and stash it in the fridge for about 1 week.

Preheat your oven and pizza stone to 450°F (230°C).

Sprinkle your countertop with a generous amount of a fifty-fifty mixture of cornmeal and flour. Push the dough down in the middle with your fingers to start forming the raised crust around the edge. Sprinkle the dough with more cornmeal and flour and flip the dough over. Stretch the crust by pulling the dough in opposite directions with both hands while you rotate the dough. When you're done, you should have a 12-inch (30 cm)-diameter dough disk of even thickness with a thicker outer crust. The outer crust should be as thick as your finger.

If you have a pizza paddle, I recommend transferring the stretched dough to a cornmeal-dusted paddle first, then adding your toppings, or prebaking your crust for 3 to 5 minutes before adding toppings. If you have some other genius way of transferring a wiggly, toppings-heavy, uncooked pizza to a flaming-hot pizza stone, though, then may the force be with you.

Add your toppings, transfer to the hot stone and bake until the crust is light brown and the toppings are hot and yummy looking (12 to 15 minutes).

Cannibal Corpse Crock-Pot

I named this faux-pulled pork recipe after my favorite American death metal band because, despite being meat-free, it looks like a straight-up massacre in your slow cooker. My fondest memory of writing this book was my mom texting me, "Made the Cannibal Corpse Crock-Pot today, OMG that sauce is SO good!" Much like Cannibal Corpse and my mom, this recipe shreds hard-core.

Serves 4 to 6

Ingredients

1 (20-ounce [567 g]) can young jackfruit in brine, drained

2 cloves of garlic, minced

1 ½ cups (360 g) organic ketchup

3 tablespoons (36 g) brown sugar

2 tablespoons (30 ml) low-sodium soy sauce or Bragg Liquid Aminos

1 tablespoon (15 ml) apple cider vinegar

1 teaspoon Sriracha chili sauce

1 teaspoon onion powder

Directions

Drain and rinse the jackfruit and squeeze out the excess water. In a medium-size bowl, whisk together the garlic, ketchup, brown sugar, soy sauce, vinegar, chili sauce and onion powder. Fold the jackfruit into the mixture and place in a slow cooker.

Cook on LOW for 6 hours, then use two forks to pull the jackfruit into shreds just like pulled pork. Serve on lettuce, or on your favorite roll—or make a BBQ Salad (page 116) if you think you're cool.

Indian Buffet Pizza

Dimo's Pizza in Chicago can make your wildest pizza fantasies come true (within reason, pervert). So when I asked them to make me a pizza inspired by Indian food, I expected something exactly as delicious as this pie turned out. Richly spiced lentils, naughty fried cauliflower and a pop of chutney atop a chewy crust make this a sophisticated pizza that even your most lowbrow friends will enjoy. If you prefer, substitute your favorite store-bought chutney for the cilantro-mint chutney.

Serves 8 to 10

Ingredients

1 pizza crust, prepared (page 100)

MADRAS LENTILS:

½ cup (96 g) dried red lentils
2 tablespoons (30 ml) olive oil
½ white onion, chopped
2 teaspoons peeled and minced fresh ginger
½ jalapeño pepper, minced
1 tablespoon (10 g) minced garlic
1 ½ teaspoons ground coriander
1 ½ teaspoons ground cumin
1 ½ teaspoons curry powder
1 cup (180 g) chopped tomatoes
4 teaspoons (21 g) tomato paste
⅓ cup (80 ml) water
Salt

CILANTRO-MINT CHUTNEY:

1 cup packed (30 g) fresh mint leaves
1 cup packed (30 g) fresh cilantro
2 tablespoons freshly squeezed lemon juice
2 tablespoons (12 g) minced fresh ginger
1 cup (230 g) vegan sour cream
½ cup (115 g) plain, unsweetened vegan soy yogurt
1 teaspoon salt

1 head of cauliflower
Oil, for frying
2 roasted red peppers, chopped

Directions

Preheat your oven to 450°F (230°C), bake the pizza crust for 3 to 5 minutes, then remove from the oven and set aside.

Make the Madras lentils: Pick through the lentils and remove any stones or debris. Rinse thoroughly under cold water. Boil the lentils in a few cups (about 500 ml) of water until they begin to soften, about 10 minutes. Drain and put aside.

Heat the oil in a large skillet over medium heat, then add the onion, ginger, jalapeño and garlic. Sauté until the onion and garlic are golden brown, 3 to 5 minutes. Add the coriander, curry, cumin, chopped tomatoes and tomato paste. Sauté for about 5 minutes, until the tomatoes are soft. Add the ⅓ cup (80 ml) of water and the lentils and bring to a boil, then reduce the heat to a simmer and cook for 10 to 15 minutes, until the lentils become soft. Add salt to taste.

Place all the ingredients for the chutney into a food processor and blend until smooth.

Break the cauliflower into small florets. Heat the oil in a deep pan and fry the florets until golden brown and tender, 7 to 8 minutes.

Spread ¼-to ½-inch (0.6 to 1.3 cm) of lentils on the crust and top with the cauliflower and roasted red peppers. Bake for 15 to 20 minutes, until the crust is golden. Top with a squirt of chutney.

Green Bean Casserole Pizza

I brought this dish to my mom's very first vegetarian Thanksgiving, along with Baked Potato Spring Rolls (page 150), and received the ultimate compliment from my little brother: "I didn't like green beans until I had this pizza." Why did it pass the brother test? I think the garlicky sauce and French-fried onions had a little something to do with it! You can prepare the topping and crust ahead of time—but wait to assemble them until guests arrive, or until you're at your final cooking destination. Or, like me, you can make one for yourself and eat it in bed while you watch *Pee-wee's Playhouse Christmas Special.*

If you can't find plain, unsweetened vegan soy yogurt in your area, whiz 1 cup (8 ounces [230 g]) of silken tofu together with 1 ½ tablespoons (25 ml) of freshly squeezed lemon juice in a food processor.

Serves 8 to 10

Ingredients

1 pizza crust (page 100)

2 tablespoons plus 1 teaspoon (42 g) salt

8 ounces (225 g) fresh green beans, trimmed and halved

2 tablespoons (28 g) vegan margarine

8 ounces (235 g) white mushrooms, sliced

½ teaspoon freshly ground black pepper

2 cloves garlic, minced

¼ teaspoon ground nutmeg

2 tablespoons (16 g) all-purpose flour

1 cup (235 ml) vegetable stock

1 cup (230 g) plain, unsweetened vegan soy yogurt

¾ cup (65 g) vegan French-fried onion pieces, plus more for topping

Directions

Preheat your oven to 450°F (230°C), bake the crust for 5 minutes, then remove from the oven and set aside.

Bring 4 quarts (3.8 L) of water and 2 tablespoons (36 g) of salt to a boil. Add the beans and cook for 5 minutes, then drain and plunge into a large bowl of ice water to stop the cooking. Drain and set aside.

Melt the margarine in a large skillet over medium-high heat. Add the mushrooms, the remaining 1 teaspoon of salt and the pepper and cook until the mushrooms start to give up some liquid, about 5 minutes.

Add the garlic and nutmeg and cook for 1 to 2 more minutes. Add the flour and stir. Cook for 1 minute, then add the vegetable stock and cook until bubbling.

Reduce the heat to medium-low and add the soy yogurt. Cook until the mixture thickens, stirring occasionally, 6 to 8 minutes.

Remove from the heat and stir in the ¾ cup (343 g) of fried onions and the green beans. Spread over the prepared pizza crust and bake for 10 to 15 minutes, until crust is golden and the toppings are hot and bubbly. Sprinkle with more fried onions to taste.

Shepherd's Pie Pizza

Some people are born to rock 'n' roll. Others are born to ride. I was born to put mashed potatoes on pizza. I've done it so many ways I can't even remember them all, but this was my favorite. Mashed potatoes, carrots, peas and plenty of savory herbs make this the only shepherd's pie you can eat while walking your dog, and for that reason, I am quite proud of it.

Serves 8 to 10

Ingredients

1 pizza crust, prepared (page 100)

"SAUCE":

1 pound (455 g) Yukon Gold potatoes
½ cup (80 g) finely chopped red onion
2 cloves garlic, minced
Splash of oil, for sautéing
¼ cup (60 ml) soy creamer
2 tablespoons (28 g) vegan margarine
½ teaspoon dried rosemary
½ teaspoon dried thyme

TOPPING:

1 carrot, diced
½ cup (75 g) peas (fresh or frozen)
½ cup (50 g) chopped cauliflower
½ cup (50 g) green beans
½ cup (35 g) sliced mushrooms
2 tablespoons (28 g) vegan margarine
2 tablespoons (16 g) all-purpose flour
½ cup (120 ml) vegetable broth
2 tablespoons (5 g) chopped fresh sage
Salt and freshly ground black pepper

Directions

Preheat your oven to 450°F (230°C), bake the pizza crust for 3 to 4 minutes, then remove from the oven, leaving the stone inside, and set aside.

Make the "sauce": Peel the potatoes and cut into ½-inch (1.3 cm) dice. Place in a saucepan and cover with cold water. Cover the pan and over high heat, bring the water to a boil. Then lower the temperature to a simmer and cook the potatoes until you can easily smash them with a fork or tongs, 15 to 20 minutes.

Sauté the onion and garlic with a splash of oil in a small pan over medium heat, until tender, 3 to 5 minutes.

Drain the potatoes and place them in a large bowl with the garlic, onion, soy creamer, margarine, rosemary and thyme. Use a potato masher to mash everything together—some lumps are fine! (You can also use a food processor, but be aware that will result in a gluey mashed potato!)

Make the topping: Steam the carrot, peas, cauliflower and green beans until tender. In a large saucepan over medium heat, combine the steamed veggies, mushrooms, margarine, flour, vegetable broth, sage, and salt and pepper to taste. Cook until a thick sauce forms, about 3 minutes, and set aside.

Spread the potato mixture over the pizza crust and top with the vegetables and salt and pepper to taste.

Bake for 15 to 20 minutes, until everything is warm and toasty.

Chicago-Style Sammich

When is a hot dog not a hot dog? When it's this sandwich! I took some of my favorite Chicago hot-dog stand flavors and piled them onto a toasty baguette for a tasty (secretly healthy) sandwich that tastes great with a side of kale chips. Try it with sport peppers (pickled hot peppers) and a squirt of mustard.

Makes 4 sammiches

Ingredients

½ batch Chee-Zee Sauce (page 160)

2 tablespoons (30 ml) vegetable oil

1 medium-size red onion, sliced

8 ounces (225 g) button mushrooms, sliced

2 to 3 cloves garlic, minced

1 pound (455 g) spinach, washed

1 medium-size tomato, diced

Celery salt

Pickle relish

4 baguettes, sliced in half and brushed with olive oil

Sport peppers (optional)

Yellow mustard (optional)

Directions

If using a freshly prepared batch of Chee-Zee Sauce, place it in the fridge to set up for a few hours so it's of spreadable consistency.

In a large skillet over medium heat, heat the oil. Add the onion and sauté for 3 minutes. Add the mushrooms and garlic and cook for 3 more minutes. Add the spinach and tomato and cook until the spinach is wilted, 2 to 3 minutes. The onion will become translucent and the mushrooms will brown. Sprinkle with celery salt and set aside. (I like to keep it over low heat so it stays warm while I move on to the next step.)

Heat a griddle over medium-high heat. Grill the baguettes until they are toasty and marked with grill marks. Spread about 2 tablespoons (28 g) of Chee-Zee Sauce on one-half of each baguette, spread 1 to 2 tablespoons (14 to 28 g) of pickle relish on the other half. Top with the vegetable mixture, and sport peppers and mustard, if desired. Smooth the baguette halves together and eat up!

Grilled Mac 'n' Cheez Sandwich

If food trucks are any indicator of popular food culture, and I believe they are, then grilled cheese sandwiches are very *in* right now. I have yet to find a grilled cheese truck, though, that offers a vegan option quite like this. Savory Chee-Zee Sauce, juicy tomatoes and fresh, earthy spinach elevate mac 'n' cheese to a full-on meal. This makes a whole mess of sandwiches, so invite your hungriest friends!

Makes 10 sandwiches

Ingredients

1 pound (455 g) macaroni
1 batch Chee-Zee Sauce (page 160)
20 slices of bread
¼ cup (57 g) vegan margarine
1 pound (455 g) spinach, washed and stems removed
1 large tomato, seeded and sliced
Salt and freshly ground black pepper

Directions

Cook the macaroni according to the package instructions, drain and stir in half of the Chee-Zee sauce. Store the other half of the batch in the refrigerator for later. Lightly spray a baking sheet with cooking spray, and spread out the mac 'n' cheez in an even layer. Place in the refrigerator for at least 1 hour to cool and set up. When the mac 'n' cheez is cold, slice it into squares that are slightly smaller than the bread you're using.

Preheat your oven to 500°F (250°C) and place a cast-iron skillet (or other ovenproof pan) inside.

Grab two slices of bread and spread margarine onto one side of each. Place one slice of bread, margarine side down, on a work surface and top with a smear of reserved Chee-Zee Sauce, a slice of mac 'n' cheez , some spinach, a slice or two of tomato, and salt and pepper. Smear some more Chee-Zee sauce on the nonmargarine side of the other slice of bread, and place it on top, margarine side up. Repeat with the remaining ingredients.

Using a pair of tongs, place the sandwiches on the hot skillet inside the oven until the bottom is toasted, then flip and cook for another few minutes, until both sides are toasted and the macaroni is warm. Slice in half and eat hot.

Thai Dagwood Sandwich

Sandwiches were *sad*wiches until I started rethinking my favorite foods in sandwich form. This sandwichy take on Thai food combines the cuisine's signature spicy peanut sauce with lots of flavorful fresh veggies and marinated tofu steaks. You'll need to open wide, but the slightly sweet sauce, meaty tofu and crispy toppings are well worth the dislocated jaw.

Makes 4 sandwiches

Ingredients

1 (14-ounce [397 g]) block firm or extra-firm tofu

Fish-free Peanut Sauce (page 159)

Coconut milk, if needed

1 tomato

1 cucumber

1 red onion

1 jalapeño pepper (optional)

8 slices of whole-grain sourdough bread (or your favorite sliced bread)

Handful of sprouts

Handful of baby spinach, washed

Directions

Drain the tofu and slice lengthwise into four "steaks." Press out the excess water. If you made your Peanut Sauce thick, thin out a 1-cup (235 ml) portion by adding coconut milk. Place the steaks inside a sealed container with the peanut sauce marinade and refrigerate for at least 30 minutes, or up to 4 hours.

Preheat your oven to 400°F (200°C), line a baking sheet with parchment paper and spray with nonstick cooking spray. Place the marinated tofu steaks on the sheet and bake for 40 minutes, flipping the steaks over halfway through cooking.

When the tofu has about 15 minutes left in the oven, rinse and dry your veggies. Slice the tomato, cucumber, onion and jalapeño (I like to cut them thin and pile them high).

Slather two pieces of bread with thick peanut sauce, add a slice of tofu and load up your sandwich with veggies. This sandwich is also yummy cold, so store those leftovers in the fridge for lunch!

BBQ Salad

Salad sucks. At least the boring bowl of flavorless green stuff I used to consider salad does. But with different tastes and textures in every bite, this hearty bowl has become a go-to dinner at my house, and we don't even care that it's full of kale. Serve it with corn bread for a soulful supper, or pack it for lunch and make everyone at the office jealous.

Serves 6

Ingredients

1 batch Cannibal Corpse Crock-Pot (page 102; see note)

Canola oil, for pan

1 small onion, diced

2 cloves garlic, minced

8 ounces (225 g) kale, stemmed and chopped

1 (15-ounce [425 g]) can red beans, drained and rinsed

2 tablespoons (30 ml) water

Juice from ½ lemon

Pinch of salt

SERVE WITH:

Cooked brown rice

Vegan Ranch Dressing (page 158)

Directions

Heat a large skillet over medium heat. Add a splash of oil, and cook the onion until translucent, about 4 minutes. Add the garlic and cook for 1 minute more, stirring often to prevent burning. Add the kale, red beans and water; cover and cook for 5 minutes, or until the kale is wilted and the beans are hot. Remove from the heat; add a squeeze of lemon and salt to taste.

Top with a generous spoonful of Cannibal Corpse Crock Pot, then drizzle with ranch dressing. Serve over warm brown rice. Also tasty served over quinoa, or on top of corn bread.

Note: The Cannibal Corpse Crock-Pot takes 6 hours to cook. Start the BBQ Salad recipe with a half-hour left on the timer.

Savory Piecrust

This is a super-simple double piecrust—perfect for potpies. I like to add herbs and spices to the crust itself to ramp up the flavor of the final dish, but it's perfectly flaky and delicious on its own. This recipe holds up well in the refrigerator, so feel free to make it a few days ahead of time so you can whip together a potpie like it ain't no thang.

Makes one 9-inch (23 cm) double piecrust

Ingredients

1 cup (125 g) all-purpose flour
1 cup (120 g) white whole wheat flour
1 teaspoon salt
⅔ cup (151 g) unhydrogenated vegetable shortening
½ cup (120 ml) very cold water

Directions

Sift together the flours and salt into a large bowl. Use a pastry blender or two forks to cut the shortening into the flour and salt until it resembles a coarse crumb. Stir in the water gradually until the mixture forms a ball. Divide in half and wrap each half in plastic. Chill for at least 15 minutes, then roll out one ball and press it into a greased 9-inch (23 cm) pie pan.

For potpies, prebake the bottom crust for 5 minutes in a preheated 425°F (220°C) oven. Remove from the oven and set aside to cool while you prepare the filling.

Quinoa Potpie

What happens when you take a dish that's yummy on its own and bake it in between flaky layers of piecrust? Magic, that's what. And also, dinner. With such bright flavors as citrus and kalamata olives, this is a hearty-yet-light entrée with surprises in every bite.

Serves 6

Ingredients

Savory piecrust (page 118)

1 large fennel bulb with greens (fronds)

1 cup (173 g) uncooked quinoa

1 ½ cups (355 ml) water

¼ teaspoon salt, plus more to taste

2 tablespoons (30 ml) olive oil

2 (15-ounce [425 g]) cans chickpeas, drained and rinsed

¾ cup (115 g) kalamata olives, halved and pitted

Zest and juice of ½ organic lemon

Zest and juice of 1 organic orange

2 tablespoons (28 g) vegan margarine

2 tablespoons (16 g) all-purpose flour

Freshly ground black pepper

½ teaspoon ground coriander

½ teaspoon ground cumin

½ cup (60 g) chopped, toasted walnuts

Directions

Preheat your oven to 425°F (220°C) and bake the bottom piecrust for 5 minutes. Remove from the oven and set aside on a wire rack.

Remove the greens from the fennel and slice the bulb into ¼-inch (6 mm) pieces. Wash and dry the fennel pieces.

In a small saucepan, bring the quinoa, water and ¼ teaspoon of salt to a boil. Reduce the heat to a simmer, cover and cook for 15 minutes. Remove from the heat and let rest for 5 minutes before fluffing with a fork.

While the quinoa cooks, heat 1 tablespoon (15 ml) of the olive oil in a large skillet over medium heat. Add the fennel bulb and for cook 10 to 15 minutes, until it becomes tender. Add the chickpeas, olives and lemon juice. Cook over medium heat for about 5 more minutes. Set aside.

Place the orange juice in a measuring cup and top off with water until you have 1 ½ cups (355 ml). In a large saucepan, melt the margarine over low heat. Stir in the flour and continue to stir until golden brown, 3 to 4 minutes. Turn up the heat to medium-high and stir in the orange juice mixture, lemon and orange zest, remaining 1 tablespoon (15 ml) of olive oil, and salt and pepper to taste. Continue to stir as it begins to thicken. Bring to a boil, then remove from the heat and stir in the quinoa, coriander and cumin.

Mix the quinoa mixture with the fennel mixture and stir in the walnuts. Spoon into the bottom crust. Roll out the top crust and place the crust over the filling, sealing the potpie by pressing edge of the top crust into edge of the bottom crust.

Cut five slits in the top crust and bake for 30 minutes. After 30 minutes, cover the edge of the potpie with aluminum foil to keep it from burning and bake for 15 more minutes. Allow the potpie to cool for 5 minutes before slicing.

Samosa Potpie

Considering I have been known to eat an entire Samosa Potpie by myself, I was tempted to call this recipe "World's Largest Samosa." Spicy potatoes and peas mixed with spinach, tomatoes and green chiles make this comfort food extra-cuddly on a chilly day, or any day, really. To verify its heartiness, I tested this recipe on my co-worker whose only request for her birthday lunch was "meat." She spent the whole day raving about it to the rest of the office. I win.

Serves 6

Ingredients

Savory piecrust (page 118)

1 large potato

1 teaspoon vegetable oil, for pan

1 cup (180 g) chopped tomato (1 large tomato)

½ cup (80 g) finely chopped onion

1 ½ teaspoons peeled and minced ginger

1 ½ teaspoons minced garlic

1 to 2 green chiles, chopped

8 ounces (225 g) chopped fresh spinach

2 tablespoons (28 g) vegan margarine

2 tablespoons (16 g) all-purpose flour

1 cup (235 ml) plain soy milk

1 tablespoon (6.3 g) curry powder

1 (1-pound [455 g]) bag frozen peas (1 ½ cups)

Pinch of salt

Directions

Preheat your oven to 425°F (220°C) and bake the bottom piecrust for 5 minutes. Remove from the oven, and set aside on a wire rack.

Poke the potato three or four times with a fork and microwave it for 10 minutes. Let cool for 5 minutes, then dice.

In a large saucepan, heat the oil over medium-low heat and cook the tomatoes and onion for 2 to 3 minutes, until onion begins to soften. Add the ginger, garlic, chiles and spinach and cook for 2 to 3 minutes, until the spinach starts to wilt, tossing the ingredients often to keep the garlic from burning.

In a small saucepan, melt the margarine over low heat. Whisk in the flour and continue to whisk until golden brown, 3 to 4 minutes. Turn up heat to medium-high and whisk in the soy milk. Cook for 2 to 3 minutes, whisking occasionally, until the mixture thickens. Turn off the heat and whisk in the curry powder.

Toss the peas, potatoes and spinach mixture in the curry mixture and add the salt. Spoon this into the prepared crust. Roll out the other crust and place over the filling, sealing the potpie by pressing the edge of the top crust into edge of the bottom crust.

Cut five slits in the top crust and bake for 30 minutes. After 30 minutes, cover the edge of the potpie with aluminum foil to keep it from burning, and bake for 15 more minutes. Allow the potpie to cool for 5 minutes before slicing.

Spaghetti Cake with Grandma Sharon's Hater-Proof Sauce

My grandma is a four-foot-ten firecracker. She'll sass you so fast you won't know what hit you, but if you're lucky, she'll make it all better with her famous spaghetti sauce. I've seen semitruck drivers go weak in the knees for it—it's 100 percent hater-proof. Grandma's sauce is the star of the show in this homey baked pasta dish that holds up well as leftovers.

Serves 10 to 12

Ingredients

SAUCE:

1 medium-size onion, peeled

2 cups (140 g) sliced baby bella mushrooms

½ to 1 cup (85 to 170 g) green or kalamata olives, pitted and halved

2 cloves garlic, minced

Oil, for pan

2 (15-ounce [425 g]) cans tomato sauce

1 (6-ounce [170 g]) can tomato paste

12 ounces (355 ml) water (use the empty tomato paste can to measure)

1 tablespoon (4 g) Italian seasoning

2 bay leaves

½ teaspoon sugar

Pinch of black pepper

Pinch of salt

CASHEW RICOTTA:

⅓ cup (48 g) raw cashews

1 (12.3-ounce [349 g]) package firm silken tofu

1 tablespoon (15 ml) freshly squeezed lemon juice

2 teaspoons salt

TOPPING:

¼ cup (28 g) bread crumbs

2 tablespoons (8 g) nutritional yeast

¼ teaspoon salt

Olive oil and bread crumbs to coat a 9 x 13-inch (23 x 33 cm) casserole dish

1 pound (455 g) spaghetti

Directions

My grandma's secret is to cut an end off the peeled onion, leaving the other end round. Cut two or three slices into the flat end, but don't cut all the way through. As the onion cooks in the sauce, it will open like a flower, flavoring the sauce without big chunks of onion. You can then decide if you want to break off pieces of onion and leave them in your final sauce, or toss the onion out.

Make the sauce: In a large saucepan, combine all the sauce ingredients, including the cut onion. Cover and simmer the sauce over medium-low heat for 1 ½ hours, stirring occasionally with a wooden spoon. When it is done cooking, remove the bay leaves from the sauce and discard.

While the sauce simmers, grind the cashews in a food processor until very fine. Add the tofu, lemon juice and salt and blend until well combined—some texture is good!

In a small bowl, mix together the bread crumbs, nutritional yeast and salt to make the topping.

Preheat your oven to 300°F (150°C) and coat your casserole dish with olive oil. Sprinkle with 1 tablespoon (7 g) of the bread crumb mixture and set aside. Cook the spaghetti al dente, according to the package directions.

Drain, but don't rinse the spaghetti and return the pasta to the pot you cooked it in. Stir in the cashew ricotta and 1 cup (235 ml) of the sauce.

Place the pasta in the casserole dish and top with about 2 tablespoons (14 g) of the bread crumb mixture. Cover with aluminum foil and bake for 30 minutes. Remove the foil and bake 15 more minutes. Cut the baked pasta into squares and serve with warm sauce poured over each slice. Sprinkle with additional bread crumb mixture or some Not-Parm (page 99).

Cut an end off the peeled onion, leaving the other end round. Cut two or three slices into the flat end, but don't cut all the way through.

Party Tip: If you prefer a chunkier pasta sauce, throw a drained can of fire-roasted tomatoes in there!

Whatsa Panzanella

In my dreams, I have a cooking show called *Snackdown* in which I prepare a meal for a famous pro wrestler of the 1980s, and we just hang out and talk about how cool they are. In this episode, I make over the classic Italian bread salad to the Southern tastes of Hillbilly Jim. It's chock-full of black-eyed peas and fresh veggies, such as beets and cucumbers, and set off with a tangy mustard dressing. Check out the Party Tips (page 127) for important notes on this recipe.

Serves 4 to 6

Ingredients

CORNBREAD:

1 tablespoon (14 g) vegan margarine
1 cup (130 g) frozen corn
2 cups (475 ml) soy milk
2 teaspoons apple cider vinegar
2 cups (340 g) cornmeal
1 cup (125 g) all-purpose flour
2 teaspoons baking powder
2 tablespoons (26 g) sugar
½ teaspoon salt
⅓ cup (80 ml) canola oil

DRESSING:

¼ cup (44 g) vegan Dijon mustard
¼ cup (81 g) agave nectar
¼ cup (60 g) Vegan Mayo (page 158)
2 tablespoons (30 ml) olive oil
2 tablespoons (30 ml) white vinegar

SALAD:

1 (14-ounce [397 g]) can black-eyed peas, drained and rinsed
½ red onion, thinly sliced
1 yellow bell pepper, seeded and cut into 1" (2.5 cm) cubes
2 tomatoes, cut into 1" (2.5 cm) cubes
1 cucumber, unpeeled, seeded and cut into ½" (1.3 cm) pieces
6 ounces (168 g) baby spinach, washed
Salt and freshly ground black pepper
1 (15-ounce [425 g]) can sliced beets, cut into 1" (2.5 cm) pieces

Directions

Preheat your oven to 350°F (180°C), and spray a 9 x 13-inch (23 x 33 cm) baking pan with cooking spray.

Make the cornbread: In a skillet over medium heat, melt the margarine, then add the corn and cook for 5 to 7 minutes, until brown flecks start to appear on the cooked kernels. Remove from the heat and let cool completely.

In a medium-size bowl, stir the vinegar into the soymilk and set aside to curdle for a minute or two while you get the other ingredients together. In a large bowl, mix together the cornmeal, flour, baking powder, sugar and salt. Add the soymilk mixture and oil to the dry ingredients and stir until just mixed. Stir in the cooled corn kernels and pour the batter into the prepared pan.

Bake for 25 to 30 minutes, or until a toothpick inserted into the center comes out clean. Let cool completely.

Once cooled, cut the cornbread into 1-inch (2.5 cm) cubes—they should be pretty dense and relatively dry. If the cornbread seems too soft, throw the cubes into a preheated 400°F (200°C) oven for about 10 minutes to dry them out.

In a small bowl, whisk together the dressing ingredients.

Make the salad: In a large bowl, mix together the black-eyed peas, onion, pepper, tomatoes, cucumber and spinach. Add the cornbread cubes and toss with the dressing. Season liberally with salt and pepper. Allow the salad to sit in the refrigerator for at least 30 minutes before serving, then toss the ingredients again. Add the beets just before serving.

Party Tips:

- This cornbread recipe is specifically made to hold up in this salad—if you eat it on its own you'll likely find it on the dense side.

- Throw the beets in last unless you like your salad bright pink.

Falafel Waffle

If it's edible, there's a 99 percent chance I've smooshed it into my waffle maker just to see what would happen. In the case of falafel, the result is a crispy-on-the-outside, soft-on-the-inside savory waffle—no deep-frying required! This hummus recipe is great with pita and veggies as well, just reduce the amount of tahini to a few tablespoons (about 30 ml).

Makes about 8 waffles

Ingredients

FALAFEL BATTER:

2 (15-ounce [425 g]) cans chickpeas, drained and rinsed

¼ cup (15 g) chopped fresh parsley

1 small onion, minced

2 cloves garlic, minced

½ teaspoon ground coriander

½ teaspoon ground cumin powder

Salt and freshly ground black pepper

1 ½ teaspoons all-purpose flour

1 teaspoon baking soda

HUMMUS "SYRUP":

1 (15-ounce [425 g]) can chickpeas, drained and rinsed

Juice from ½ lemon

¼ cup (60 g) tahini

¼ cup (60 ml) olive oil

1 to 2 cloves garlic

Pinch of salt

TOPPING:

1 medium-size cucumber, diced

1 large tomato, diced

Juice from ½ lemon

1 tablespoon (15 ml) olive oil

Salt and freshly ground black pepper

Directions

To make the falafel batter, use a food processor to blend the chickpeas, parsley, onion and garlic until there are no large chunks (small chunks are fine; they give the falafel texture)—you might need to do this in two or three batches. Transfer this mixture to a large bowl and stir in the coriander, cumin, salt, pepper, flour and baking soda. Refrigerate for at least 1 hour.

While that sets up, make the hummus "syrup." Combine all the ingredients in a food processor until you have a creamy texture. It should be looser than a typical hummus, so you can pipe it on top of the cooked waffle.

Following the manufacturer's directions, preheat your waffle maker and spray it with cooking spray. If you can choose a temperature, go with medium. Spoon about ⅓ cup (70 g) of the falafel batter into each cavity and close the cover. Cook for 12 to 15 minutes, until the outside is crispy and lightly browned.

Make the topping: Toss the cucumber and tomato in the lemon juice and olive oil and season to taste with salt and pepper.

Top the falafel waffle with hummus and a generous pile of tomato and cucumber. Serve warm.

Pretzel Dogs of the Dead

Now, at first it might seem as if government-issue crackers or Spam would be a more suitable *Dawn of the Dead*–inspired recipe, but when I think *DotD*, I think late-'70s mall like the one it was filmed in. And when I think late-'70s mall, I think of food courts—I can't pass a mall food court without gazing longingly at the pretzel dogs and wishing aloud that they were somehow vegan. Wish no more, my friends—I present to you homemade mall food. This recipe makes one entire package of veggie dogs. To feed invading biker gangs, you may want to double or triple this recipe.

Makes 6 to 8 pretzel dogs

Ingredients

1 ½ cups (355 ml) warm water

1 tablespoon (13 g) sugar

2 teaspoons kosher salt

1 (2 ¼-teaspoon [9 g]) package active dry yeast

4 ½ cups (562 g) all-purpose flour

2 tablespoons (28 g) vegan margarine, melted

1 (12-ounce [340 g]) package veggie dogs

1 cup (235 ml) warm water (about 110°F [43°C])

1 tablespoon (4.6 g) baking soda

1 to 2 tablespoons (14 to 28 g) vegan margarine, melted

Kosher or pretzel salt, to finish

Directions

Combine the water, sugar and kosher salt in the bowl of a stand mixer and sprinkle the yeast on top. Allow to sit for 5 minutes, or until the mixture begins to foam. Add the flour and margarine and, using the dough hook attachment, mix on low speed until well combined. Change to medium speed and knead until the dough is smooth and pulls away from the side of the bowl, 4 to 5 minutes. Remove the dough from the bowl, clean the bowl and then oil it well with vegetable oil.

Return the dough to the bowl, cover with plastic wrap and set in a warm place for 50 to 55 minutes, or until the dough has doubled in size.

Preheat your oven to 450°F (230°C). Once the dough has risen, pinch off golf-ball-size pieces and roll them into 12-inch (30 cm) ropes. You might want to flour your hands and the surface you're rolling on because this dough is sticky. Wrap each veggie dog in the dough and place on a parchment paper–lined cookie sheet. (I use a silicone mat, which makes my pretzel dogs fancy *and* French.) Mix warm water and baking soda together. Brush each wrapped dog with this mixture and then bake for 10 minutes, or until golden brown.

Brush each baked dog with melted margarine and sprinkle with kosher salt.

Chapter 4

Snack Time

I wrote this chapter, and really, all of these chapters, with partying in mind. You might be down to cook a four-course dinner for a group of friends, but I'd rather put a bunch of snacks on the table and let the *RoboCop* marathon begin! (He wears a jet-pack in *RoboCop 3!*)

But snacks are not limited to partying alone. These not-quite-entrées can also serve as appetizers— you know, predinner snacks. Serve Mac 'n' Cheez Ballz before diving into a BBQ Salad, or Baked Potato Spring Rolls prior to a Green Bean Casserole Pizza. Many of these recipes can be prepared ahead of time and then simply reheated when chow time is upon you.

Try my healthy Game Day Dip while you pretend to understand football, or make a batch of Ca-razy Caprese on Toast to hold you over until lunch. And don't miss my suggestions for eating everything on your plate, including your plate!

Pizza Cupcakes

Technically these are muffins, or possibly even biscuits. But after one bite of these savory little snack cups, I doubt anyone will be too worried about semantics. Make them mini and serve them with marinara as a bite-size appetizer or go big and serve them with a pasta dish. I use a pastry-filling tip to inject marinara directly into the center of mine.

Makes 10 cupcakes

Ingredients

1 cup (235 ml) soy milk

¼ cup (60 ml) vegetable oil

¼ cup (60 g) blended silken tofu

2 cups (250 g) all-purpose flour

¼ cup (25 g) Not-Parm (page 99), plus more for topping

¼ cup (10 g) chopped fresh basil leaves

2 ½ teaspoons baking powder

1 teaspoon Italian seasoning

¼ teaspoon salt

½ cup (55 g) chopped sun-dried tomatoes in olive oil, drained

½ cup (85 g) kalamata olives, chopped

Marinara or pizza sauce, for dipping (optional)

Directions

Preheat your oven to 400°F (200°C) and grease the bottoms of a muffin pan. In a large bowl, beat together the soy milk, oil and tofu. Stir in the flour, Not-Parm, basil, baking powder, Italian seasoning and salt until just moistened. Fold in the tomatoes and olives and fill baking cups with batter. Sprinkle the tops with more Not-Parm and bake for 18 to 20 minutes. Serve warm.

Nacho Cupcakes

Again, technically this is a muffin. I think I just enjoy the horrified look on people's faces when I say things like, "Have you tried the nacho cupcake?" Sadistic. Anyway, serve these with a bean salad and a side of guacamole and you've got yourself a fiesta. Better yet, bake the muffins and let your guests top their own!

Makes 12 cupcakes

Ingredients

1 cup (235 ml) soy milk

1 teaspoon apple cider vinegar

1 cup (125 g) all-purpose flour

¾ cup (127 g) yellow cornmeal

1 tablespoon (14 g) baking powder

½ teaspoon salt

½ teaspoon freshly ground black pepper

2 medium-size jalapeños, diced with seeds

⅓ cup (50 g) corn kernels (thawed, if frozen)

¼ cup (60 g) blended silken tofu

⅓ cup (67 g) sugar

2 tablespoons (30 ml) vegetable oil

Unhydrogenated vegetable shortening, for greasing pan

TOPPINGS:

1 (15-ounce [425 g]) can refried beans

Sliced olives

Additional jalapeño slices, ground seitan, guacamole, etc. (optional)

Tortilla chips

Nacho Chee-Zee Sauce (page 161)

Directions

Preheat your oven to 400°F (200°C) and grease a twelve-cup muffin pan with shortening.

In a measuring cup, combine the soy milk and apple cider vinegar and set aside to curdle for a few minutes while you prepare the other ingredients. In a medium-size bowl, combine the flour, cornmeal, baking powder, salt and pepper. In another bowl, whisk together the soy milk mixture, jalapeños, corn, tofu, sugar and oil. Add to the dry ingredients and stir until just combined.

Fill the prepared muffin cups two-thirds full. Bake until golden brown and a toothpick inserted into the center comes out clean, 15 to 20 minutes. Remove from the pan and let cool completely on wire rack.

To nacho-fy the "cupcakes": Warm the refried beans on your stovetop; spread a layer of beans on top of each muffin. Sprinkle with olives and additional peppers or other toppings, if desired. Top it with a tortilla chip, serve with Nacho Chee-Zee Sauce, and get ready to party.

Mac 'n' Cheez Ballz

Fancy grocery stores refer to these as "croquettes" but that's nowhere near as funny as "ballz." Chee-Zee macaroni takes a dunk in a zesty batter and a dip in the deep fryer to make a crispy snack with a warm and creamy filling. There's a lot of downtime while making these, so make sure to fit in important activities, such as one-armed push-ups, hashtagging things on Instagram and practicing your air guitar solo while you wait. You can make these ahead of time and then reheat them in a 400°F (200°C) oven.

Makes about 20 pieces

Ingredients

1 pound (455 g) macaroni
1 batch Chee-Zee Sauce (page 160)
Canola oil, for frying
1 cup (125 g) self-rising flour
⅔ cup (100 g) cornstarch
1 teaspoon garlic powder
Pinch of paprika
1 cup (235 ml) cold water
2 tablespoons (30 ml) canola oil, warmed in the microwave for a few seconds
1 tablespoon + 1 teaspoon (18 g) baking powder

Directions

Cook the macaroni according to the package instructions, drain and stir in the Chee-Zee sauce. Transfer to a casserole dish and place in the refrigerator for 2 hours to cool and set up. Scoop golf-ball-size scoops of cooled mac 'n' cheez onto a baking sheet lined with waxed paper and place in the freezer for 2 more hours.

Heat the frying oil to 350°F (180°C) in a large pan, or fill a deep fryer with oil as directed by the manufacturer. If you don't have a thermometer, you can test the oil by sticking a wooden chopstick or the end of a wooden spoon about 1 inch (2.5 cm) deep into the oil. If you see bubbles, the oil is hot enough for frying.

Whisk the flour, cornstarch, garlic powder and paprika together, then add the water. Mix in the warm canola oil, then the baking powder. Use a fork to dip the frozen mac 'n' cheez balls in the batter, allowing the excess to drip off. Add the battered balls (heh) one or two at a time to the hot oil. Adding too many frozen items to the oil will lower the temperature and make everything greasy and soggy. Fry for 2 to 3 minutes until golden brown, then flip if necessary and fry for another 2 to 3 minutes. Drain on paper towels before serving hot.

Dip your balls (heh) in marinara sauce or in Vegan Ranch (page 158).

Totchos

Here I'm utilizing the potato's most impressive form—the tot—only this time the tot's going macho with the help of refried beans and spicy Nacho Chee-Zee Sauce. Some may argue that making nachos you have to eat with a fork defeats the purpose of nachos, so don't invite those people over and you won't have to worry about it. Anyway, the more of these spicy tots, tangy toppings and zesty Nacho Chee-Zee Sauce you get to keep for yourself, the happier you will be!

Serves 6 to 8

Ingredients

1 batch Nacho Chee-Zee Sauce
(page 161)

1 (20- to 32-ounce [567 to 905 g])
bag frozen Tater Tots

TACO SEASONING:

1 ½ teaspoons chili powder

1 teaspoon ground cumin

1 teaspoon salt

1 teaspoon freshly ground black pepper

¼ teaspoon garlic powder

¼ teaspoon onion powder

¼ teaspoon crushed red pepper flakes

¼ teaspoon dried oregano

1 (15-ounce [425 g]) can vegetarian
refried beans

1 tomato, diced (optional)

Black olives, pitted and sliced
(optional)

Directions

Prepare the Nacho Chee-Zee Sauce and keep warm (or prepare ahead of time and reheat before serving).

Preheat the oven according to the directions on the Tater Tots package. In a small bowl, mix together all of the taco seasoning ingredients. Open the top of the Tater Tot bag, pour in about one-quarter of the taco seasoning mix, hold the top of the bag closed and shake. Add the remaining seasoning gradually, shaking after each addition, until the tots are coated. Place the tots in a single layer on a baking sheet, and bake according to the package directions. (I give them a few extra minutes so they're nice and crunchy).

While the Tater Tots bake, warm up the refried beans in a small saucepan.

When the tots are baked, remove them from the oven and place them on a large serving dish. Top with refried beans, Nacho Chee-Zee Sauce and the optional nacho toppings of your choice.

Party Tip: Make it a meal by pouring a can of chili over the whole mess before adding Nacho Chee-Zee Sauce.

OCD Chips 'n' Dip

If watching your guests reach their grubby hands into the chip bowl time and time again makes you cringe, this recipe will solve your germophobe woes. I give you a hearty serving of chunky avocado salsa (with just a hint of cool mint) nestled inside its own crispy chip bowl, with all possibility of double-dipping eliminated.

Makes 12 individual bowls

Ingredients

12 Mini Tortilla Bowls (page 153)

⅔ cup (150 g) Vegan Mayo (page 158) or store-bought

Juice of 1 lime

2 tablespoons (12 g) finely chopped fresh mint

1 clove garlic, grated

¼ teaspoon salt

Splash of hot sauce

1 small red onion, finely chopped

2 plum tomatoes, seeded and diced

2 ripe avocados, peeled, pitted and diced

Directions

Prepare the Mini Tortilla Bowls as directed on page 153, remove from the oven and allow to cool.

In a large bowl, stir together the vegan mayo, lime juice, mint, garlic, salt and hot sauce to taste. Gently stir in the onion, tomatoes and avocado until coated. Divide the avocado mixture among the tortilla bowls and serve immediately.

Party Tip: Look for vegan wonton wrappers at the Asian grocery store and bake them pressed into mini muffin pans instead of using Mini Tortilla Bowls, for bite-size appetizers.

Game Day Dip

I shock and horrify my punk rock friends with my genuine love of football. Yes, they are the same jocks who laughed at us and called us names in high school, but I forgive them because I love violence and spinach dip. You can't properly watch the game with your buddies without a heaping bowl of tangy spinach dip, and being vegan is no excuse. Here I've added kale for additional green power, and replaced soup mix with a couple of MSG-free seasonings.

Serves 6

Ingredients

1 (12.3-ounce [349 g]) package silken tofu

¼ cup (60 ml) freshly squeezed lemon juice (about 1 ½ lemons)

¼ cup (40 g) roughly chopped red onion

2 cloves garlic, roughly chopped

1 teaspoon onion powder

1 teaspoon Vegeta seasoning

1 cup packed (55 g) chopped spinach

1 cup packed (55 g) washed, stemmed and chopped curly kale leaves

½ cup (62 g) chopped water chestnuts

Freshly ground black pepper

Directions

In a food processor, blend the tofu, lemon juice, onion, garlic, onion powder and Vegeta seasoning until smooth. Add the spinach, kale and water chestnuts and pulse three or four times (you want chunks and bumps). Cover the bowl with plastic wrap and refrigerate for at least 2 hours.

Serve with bread, pita chips or veggie sticks.

Party Tips:

- I like to use Vegeta seasoning in my Mac 'n' Yeast (page 162) as well. If you can't find it, use your favorite seasoned salt or celery salt instead.

- Jazz up your dip as you see fit by adding red bell peppers, green onions, or any other flavorful veggies, herbs and seasonings you like!

Ca-razy Caprese on Toast

Caprese is one of the simplest, tastiest salads known to man—but the star of the show is fresh mozzarella, which vegan scientists have yet to perfect. Rather than fake the funk, I've swapped mozzarella for avocado, a.k.a. nature's mozzarella. Paired with aromatic basil leaves, fresh tomatoes and sweet, tangy balsamic vinegar, the avocados' creamy texture is spot-on. Avocados start to turn brown quickly, so make the spread right before serving.

Makes about 30 pieces

Ingredients

1 baguette loaf, cut into ½" (1.3 cm)-thick slices

¼ cup (60 ml) olive oil

Salt and freshly ground black pepper

5 plum tomatoes, diced

2 to 3 ripe avocados, peeled, pitted and mashed

1 bunch fresh basil leaves, stemmed and chopped

¼ cup (60 ml) balsamic vinegar (optional)

Directions

Preheat your oven to 450°F (230°C).

Brush one side of the sliced baguette with olive oil and arrange oil side up on a baking sheet. Sprinkle with salt and bake until the bread is golden and crisp, about 5 minutes.

While the bread toasts, stir the tomatoes and basil into the mashed avocado (Italian guacamole!)

Spread the avocado mixture on each piece of toast and then a drizzle of balsamic vinegar. Add salt and pepper to taste.

Party Tip: If you don't plan on making out with anyone later, rub each slice of bread with a raw garlic clove before toasting it.

Chicago Mix Popcorn

Chicago is best-known for its deep-dish pizzas and no-ketchup-on-hot dogs rule—but avid Chicagophiles will tell you that Chicago Mix popcorn is this city's best-kept snack secret. There's something so deliciously wrong about the combination of cheese powder and crunchy caramel corn—you want to say no, but you just can't! I've re-created the salty, cheesy, sweet flavor here with a dairy-free caramel and a cheese-less cheese powder!

Makes about 5 cups (40 g)

Ingredients

CHEE-ZEE POPCORN:

½ cup (100 g) unpopped popcorn kernels

Oil, for popping

Olive oil cooking spray

¼ cup (16 g) nutritional yeast

1 teaspoon salt

CARAMEL:

½ cup (100 g) granulated sugar

½ cup (75 g) light brown sugar

¼ cup (60 ml) light corn syrup

1 ½ tablespoons (25 ml) water

1 ½ tablespoons (21 g) vegan margarine

½ teaspoon vanilla extract

¼ teaspoon baking soda

Directions

Pop the popcorn in your preferred method—but don't use microwave popcorn, it won't stay crunchy. I add about 3 tablespoons (45 ml) of oil to a large saucepan and heat it on medium-high heat. Drop a few kernels in and wait for them to pop. Once they pop, add the rest of the kernels, cover and remove from the heat for about 30 seconds so they all get brought to near-popping temperature at the same time. Return the pan to the heat, and shake the pan over the burner to prevent the popcorn from burning. Once it starts popping rapidly, remove the lid to release steam. Once you have to wait several seconds between pops, turn off the heat and remove the pan from the burner.

Dump the popcorn into a really big bowl, and lightly spray it with olive oil spray. Toss sprayed popcorn with nutritional yeast and salt, spraying more oil if needed. Set aside.

Line a baking sheet with waxed paper and set aside.

Make the caramel: In a medium-size saucepan over medium heat, combine the sugars, corn syrup and water and stir until the sugar is melted. Bring the mixture to a low boil and cook it until it becomes amber in color—8 to 10 minutes. Stir occasionally to prevent burning. Remove from the heat and stir in the vanilla, margarine and baking soda. Working quickly, pour the hot caramel over the popcorn and stir to coat.

Spread on the waxed paper and allow to cool completely, about 20 minutes.

Baked Potato Spring Rolls

No one ever called baked potatoes party food. Delicious as they are, they're just awkward to eat while standing around a crowded room. I took all the yummy flavors of baked potatoes and wrapped them up tight in a crunchy spring roll wrapper so you can eat them with one hand. Plus, they can be made ahead of time and frozen, then warmed up in the oven when guests arrive. Party hard.

Makes about 20 spring rolls

Ingredients

1 pound (455 g) russet potatoes, peeled and chopped into large chunks

¼ to ½ cup (60 to 120 ml) soy creamer

¼ cup (16 g) nutritional yeast

2 tablespoons (28 g) vegan margarine

Salt and freshly ground black pepper

¼ cup (25 g) chopped green onions

½ cup (45 g) vegan bacon (optional, see Party Tip)

1 (11-ounce [312 g]) package spring roll wrappers

Canola oil, for frying

¼ cup (60 ml) Vegan Ranch Dip (page 158)

Directions

Place the potato chunks into a large pan and cover with water. Bring the water to a boil, then reduce the heat to a simmer and cook the potatoes for 15 to 20 minutes, or until you can easily smash them with a fork. When the potatoes are done, drain and mash them together with the nutritional yeast, margarine and ¼ cup (60 ml) of soy creamer—mash until smooth and add salt and pepper to taste. You want a pretty loose mash, so add more creamer, if needed. Stir in the green onions. If you're going with the bacony option, add that now, too. (See Party Tip for more.)

Prep the spring roll wrappers as directed on the package. Add about 2 tablespoons (28 g) of the mashed potato mixture diagonally, near one corner of wrapper. Make an envelope by folding the other two corners over the filling and then pulling up the corner near the filling. Roll toward the last corner, and use a little water to stick the roll closed.

Place the assembled rolls on a baking sheet covered in waxed paper, leaving a little space between them so they don't stick together. Freeze the assembled rolls for at least 2 hours; this keeps them from falling apart in the fryer. You can also store them frozen until you're ready to fry them at a later date.

Pour 4 inches (10 cm) of oil into a deep pan. Heat the oil until it is about 350°F (180°C). If you don't have a thermometer, you can test the oil by sticking a wooden chopstick or the end of a wooden spoon about 1 inch (2.5 cm) deep into the oil. If you see bubbles, the oil is hot enough for frying.

Add two or three spring rolls to the oil at a time and cook for 4 to 5 minutes, or until golden on both sides. Set the finished spring rolls on paper towels to drain. If desired, you can fry the rolls ahead of time, then reheat them in a preheated 350°F (180°C) oven before serving.

Slice the rolls in half and serve with Vegan Ranch Dip (page 158).

Party Tip: Want to add some smoky bacon flavor? Stir ½ cup (40 g) of cooked veggie bacon, imitation bacon bits or chopped pieces of your favorite vegan deli slices into the mashed potatoes, along with the green onions. Quickly fry the deli slices in a bit of oil to give them some crunch.

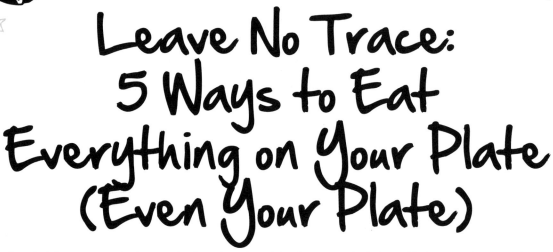

Leave No Trace: 5 Ways to Eat Everything on Your Plate (Even Your Plate)

As a kid, I ate every meal using the bread to shovel food onto my fork; I would alternate between bites of dinner and bites of bread. My dad called it my edible napkin, which inspired these ideas for eating everything on your plate, including your plate.

Mashed Potato Bowl

A certain fast-food fried chicken chain caught a lot of flack when it introduced a fat-and-calorie-bomb with a similar name. No worries, though, because this bowl can be filled with lots of healthy stuff, such as veggie chili or BBQ Salad (page 116).

Serves 4 to 6

Ingredients

1 ½ pounds (680 g) Yukon Gold potatoes, peeled
½ teaspoon salt
¼ cup (60 ml) soy creamer
2 tablespoons (28 g) vegan margarine
Salt and freshly ground black pepper

Directions

Cut the potatoes into a ½-inch (1.3 cm) dice and place in a saucepan. Add the salt and cover the potatoes with water. Bring to a boil, then reduce the heat and simmer, covered, for 15 to 20 minutes, or until a fork can easily be poked into them.

Drain the potatoes and place in a heatproof bowl. Add the soy creamer and margarine, and use potato masher to mash the potatoes. Then use a wooden spoon to stir everything together. Add salt and pepper to taste.

Scoop a pile of mashed potatoes onto a plate and use a large spoon to create a well in the center. Fill the bowl with anything you like!

Mini Tortilla Bowls

Arguably the best part of ordering the taco salad at a Mexican restaurant is the huge, crunchy tortilla bowl it comes in. Make your own mini versions at home and fill them with Totchos (page 141) or use them for OCD Chips 'n' Dip (page 142).

Makes 12 bowls

Ingredients

1 (8.2-ounce [232 g]) package small (6" [15 cm]-diameter) flour tortillas
Water
Pinch of salt

Directions

Preheat your oven to 375°F (190°C) and sprinkle the tortillas with enough water to make a little salt stick to each one.

Flip a muffin tin upside down and nestle the tortillas between the cups, shaping them into small bowls. Bake for 8 to 10 minutes, until golden and crispy.

For full-size tortilla bowls, sprinkle large flour tortillas with water and salt, then bake them for 8 to 10 minutes on overturned oven-safe cups or jars.

Squash Bowl

Baked acorn squash comes in its own biodegradable bowl—how's that for convenience? After you eat the delicious guts, you can shove the rind in your compost or, depending on your neighbor situation, chuck it in your yard. But don't stop there—fill it with couscous and your favorite veggies and seasonings for a complete meal. (Omit the sugar if you're filling it with savory stuff!)

Makes 2 bowls

Ingredients

1 acorn squash
1 tablespoon (14 g) vegan margarine
2 tablespoons (18 g) brown sugar
Pinch of salt

Directions

Preheat your oven to 400°F (200°C). Using a large knife, cut the squash in half from stem to end. Scoop out and discard the seeds.

Score the insides with a knife several times, and place cut side up on a rimmed baking sheet. Add ¼ inch (6 mm) of water to the bottom of the baking sheet to keep the squash moist while it cooks.

Coat the flesh with margarine (1 ½ teaspoons on each half) and sprinkle with salt. Add 1 tablespoon (9 g) of brown sugar to the cavity of each half and bake for 1 hour, or until the flesh is soft and slightly browned. Let cool for 5 minutes before eating.

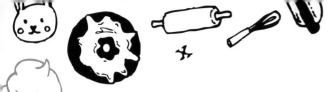

Chocolate Cups

Tell me, what doesn't taste better with chocolate? Tomato soup, you say? Okay, well, maybe you're right. But these easy, mini chocolate cups fancy-up any dessert. Fill them with Vanilla Soy Latte Granita (page 84) or anything else you can imagine!

Makes 16 chocolate cups

Ingredients

16 water balloons, plus more in case you break a few
1 ½ pounds (680 g) vegan chocolate, chopped

Directions

Blow the balloons up so they're slightly larger than a large egg. Wash each balloon with soap and water, dry them and set them aside.

Line a few baking sheets with waxed paper and keep them close to where you'll be working with the chocolate.

Place ¾ pound (340 g) of chopped chocolate in a metal bowl atop a pot of simmering water. Once the chocolate has melted, remove it from the heat and set aside to cool for 5 minutes.

Holding the knot, dip the bottom of one balloon into the chocolate—almost halfway up the balloon. Remove from the chocolate and hold for about 5 seconds, then dip the same balloon again.

Set the dipped balloon on the lined baking sheet; the chocolate will form a little foot around the bottom. You should be able to coat eight balloons before you need to melt your remaining ¾ pound (340 g) of chocolate to begin again.

Allow the chocolate to cool completely, about an hour. Then clip the tip of the balloon with scissors, letting the air out without popping it. (Popping might break the cup.)

If the popped balloons are sticking inside cups, place the cups in the freezer for a few minutes, then pull the balloons out of the frozen cups. Store the cups in the freezer or refrigerator until ready to use.

Birdseed Plate

I used to work for a company that sold eco-friendly everything. After three years of dealing with customer requests for a more sustainable paper plate, I came up with this idea that, for whatever reason, never took off.

Makes 1 plate

Ingredients

1 all-natural, unbleached, hippie-dippie paper plate
¼ cup (65 g) all-natural peanut butter
1 cup (140 g) birdseed

Directions

Coat the bottom of each paper plate with peanut butter, then dip into birdseed. Eat your meal outside because it will be incredibly messy and your hands will be sticky. When you're finished, throw the plate in the grass and watch the birds go nuts for it. *This may or may not be a terrible idea.*

Chapter 5

On the Side

What's a sandwich without a side of chips? What's a salad without ranch dressing? Macaroni without cheese? These are the questions that keep me up at night. A nightmare scenario where I am forced to forgo the crunchy, salty or cheesy side dish I crave simply because I'm trying to eat healthy.

The nightmare is over, because I have come up with Five Sauces and Dips You'll Always Use—from Vegan Mayo to Nacho Chee-Zee Sauce. Likewise, I have found five nonboring ways to enjoy kale chips— the bright green alternative to potato chips.

My Stuffin' Muffins and Crouching Corn Bread, Hidden Broccoli are perfect for sopping up extra sauce or scooping up fresh salads, and Mac 'n' Yeast is the vegan mac 'n' cheese with a funny name you didn't know you loved.

5 Sauces and Dips You'll Always Use

Vegan Mayo, Ranch Dip & Dressing

This is a simple recipe you can zip together on a weekend and store in the fridge for up to two weeks. Plus, it's a two-for-one because to make vegan ranch dressing delicious, you must first make vegan mayo! This recipe makes a thick dressing that can also be used as a dip—to thin it out, just add a splash of unsweetened soy milk.

Makes about 2 cups (450 g)

Ingredients

VEGAN MAYO:

1 (12.3-ounce [349 g]) package firm silken tofu

½ cup (71 g) raw cashews (see note)

3 tablespoons freshly squeezed lemon juice

2 tablespoons (30 ml) olive oil

1 teaspoon prepared yellow mustard

⅛ teaspoon granulated onion powder

Salt

RANCH DRESSING:

2 tablespoons (8 g) minced fresh dill

1 tablespoon (3 g) minced fresh chives

1 ½ teaspoons garlic powder

1 teaspoon onion powder

½ teaspoon freshly ground black pepper

¼ teaspoon paprika

Directions

Drain the water from the tofu. Place all the ingredients in a high-speed blender and blend until smooth, scraping down the sides as necessary.

To transform your mayo into ranch dressing, add the ranch dressing ingredients to the mixture and blend again until smooth.

Chill until ready to use.

Note: To make this recipe in a food processor or regular blender, soak the cashews in water for 2 to 3 hours to soften them, or use ⅓ cup (86 g) of cashew butter instead of the cashews and process until smooth.

Fish-free Peanut Sauce

My apologies to ketchup and mustard, but peanut sauce is my favorite condiment by far. It makes a delicious dip for vegetables and fried tofu—in fact, you can even dunk your toast in it. Use it as a marinade, slather it on a sandwich or just eat it with a spoon when no one's looking.

Makes about 2 cups (475 ml)

Ingredients

1 cup (145 g) unsalted dry-roasted peanuts

⅓ cup (80 ml) water

2 cloves garlic, minced

2 teaspoons sesame oil

1 to 2 tablespoons (9 to 18 g) brown sugar, to taste

1 ½ to 2 tablespoons Bragg Amino Acids or soy sauce

2 tablespoons (30 ml) freshly squeezed lime juice

1 teaspoon hot chili sauce (Huy Fong Sriracha)

⅓ cup (80 ml) coconut milk, or more if using as a marinade

Directions

Place all the ingredients into a food processor and blend until smooth. Taste and add more Bragg if you'd like it a little saltier, or more sugar if it's too salty. If using as a marinade, add more coconut milk until you achieve the desired consistency. This sauce thickens as it sits.

No-Honey Mustard

Whether or not you're sympathetic to the plight of the honey bee, you have to admit that honey (bee barf) is kind of gross. And yet, there's nothing better to dunk Mac 'n' Cheez Ballz (page 138) or plain old pretzels in than honey mustard. Relax; here's a barf-free mustard dip that will get you buzzing.

Ingredients

MIX EQUAL PARTS:

Vegan Mayo (page 158)

Dijon mustard

Agave nectar

Plus, a pinch of salt

Directions

Combine the ingredients in a small bowl—I usually make about 1 cup (240 g), so that's ⅓ cup (75 g) of mayo, ⅓ cup (58 g) of mustard, and ⅓ cup [108 g] of agave. Refrigerate for about an hour; it will thicken once it's cold.

Chee-Zee Sauce

This all-purpose cheesy sauce calls for a whole lotta nutritional yeast. Nutritional yeast is a deactivated yeast grown on cane and beet molasses—but don't let that discourage you. After all, where would bread or beer be without yeast? Nutritional yeast is a complete protein, rich in B-complex vitamins and its nutty, cheesy flavor has made it a staple in vegan pantries worldwide.

Makes about 4 cups (946 ml)

Ingredients

6 tablespoons (85 g) vegan margarine

⅓ cup (42 g) all-purpose flour

2 ½ cups (570 ml) boiling water

1 tablespoon (15 ml) soy sauce or Bragg Liquid Aminos

2 cups (128 g) nutritional yeast

1 teaspoon seasoned salt

1 teaspoon garlic powder

1 teaspoon onion powder

1 tablespoon (11 g) prepared yellow mustard

Directions

In a large saucepan, melt the margarine over medium heat. Whisk in the flour until smooth and bubbly. Add the boiling water and soy sauce and whisk until smooth. Add the nutritional yeast and whisk until completely smooth. Stir in the seasoned salt, garlic and onion powders, and mustard. Remove from the heat.

Party Tips:

- If you're making pasta or another dish that calls for melted cheese, use this recipe hot. You can also refrigerate it for a few hours to use as a spread. To reheat, add a splash of water and heat the Chee-Zee Sauce over medium-low heat just until hot.

- Sometimes you only need a little cheese. To make a half batch of Chee-Zee Sauce, use the following measurements: 3 tablespoons (43 g) of vegan margarine; 2 tablespoons + 2 teaspoons (21 g) of all-purpose flour; 1 ¼ cups (295 ml) of boiling water; 1 ½ teaspoons of soy sauce; 1 cup (64 g) of nutritional yeast; ½ teaspoon each of seasoned salt, garlic powder and onion powder; and 1 ½ teaspoons of prepared yellow mustard.

Nacho Chee-Zee Sauce

This zesty version of Chee-Zee Sauce has just enough heat to let you know you're eating nacho "cheese," but not enough to blow your taste buds off. Of course, if you're looking to make your mouth explode, just keep piling on the chipotle peppers and don't come crying to me when your body rebels against you.

Makes 3 cups (700 g)

Ingredients

1 ½ teaspoons salt

2 cups (475 ml) warm water (about 100°F [38°C])

¼ cup (36 g) raw cashews

1 cup (64 g) nutritional yeast

1 chipotle pepper in adobo sauce, diced, or more to taste

2 tablespoons (19 g) cornstarch

1 tablespoon (14 ml) freshly squeezed lemon juice

½ teaspoon onion powder

½ teaspoon garlic powder

Directions

Dissolve the salt in the warm water. Add the cashews to the water and soak for 1 hour.

Place all the ingredients, including the cashews and their soaking water, in a food processor and blend until smooth. Visible specks of pepper are A-OK! Taste at this point and decide if you want to add more chipotle peppers—remember, a little goes a long way.

Transfer to a saucepan and cook over medium heat, whisking occasionally, until thickened, about 10 minutes. Remove from the heat.

Mac 'n' Yeast

Don't run away yet; you're about to learn about the wonders of nutritional yeast! The name is creepy, but it's actually a great vegan source of vitamin B_{12} that happens to taste just like cheese! This recipe was handed down to me by my friend Eric, owner of Refuge Skate Shop in Detroit. He's a longtime vegan and snack master extraordinaire. Just like a baked mac 'n' cheese made with sharp cheddar, this pasta dish is creamy, cheesy and has a touch of tangy zip. I can't even tell you how many times I've tricked my family into eating this at potlucks—no one ever knew it was vegan!

Serves 8

Ingredients

1 pound (455 g) macaroni (or your preferred pasta)
1 batch Chee-Zee Sauce (page 160)
Pinch of paprika
Bread crumbs

Directions

Preheat your oven to 350°F (180°C). Cook the macaroni halfway (whatever time the package instructs, halve it.) Drain and set aside. Prepare the Chee-Zee Sauce and divide in half. Mix one-half with the noodles and transfer to a casserole dish. Pour the remaining sauce on top and sprinkle with paprika and bread crumbs. Bake for 25 minutes and finish in a broiler for 2 to 3 minutes, until crispy and browned.

Deep-fried Creamed Corn

Shout out to Superdawg Drive-In! You can make these ahead of time, then reheat them in a 400°F (200°C) oven. Serve them with Vegan Ranch (page 158) or No-Honey Mustard (page 159). These fritters are sweet—you could even top them with a dusting of confectioners' sugar. For a more savory option, omit the sugar and throw ½ cup (80 g) of chopped white onion into the pan before adding the corn.

Makes about 15 pieces

Ingredients

¼ cup (57 g) vegan margarine

1 (16-ounce [455 g]) package frozen whole kernel corn

½ cup (120 ml) plain soy creamer

1 teaspoon sugar

Salt and freshly ground black pepper

¼ cup (28 g) bread crumbs or crushed vegan crackers

2 cups (250 g) all-purpose flour

½ teaspoon garlic powder

¼ teaspoon onion powder

1 cup (235 ml) beer (see note)

Oil, for frying

Directions

Melt the margarine in a large skillet over medium heat. Add the frozen corn and cook until mostly thawed. Add the soy creamer and sugar, then salt and pepper to taste.

Continue cooking over medium heat, stirring frequently to prevent the creamer from burning, for 10 to 15 minutes, until the sauce is thickened. Stir in the bread crumbs, remove from the heat and let cool for 10 to 15 minutes.

Line a baking sheet with waxed paper, drop spoonfuls of the corn mixture onto the sheet, and freeze until firm, about 3 hours.

Mix 1 cup (125 g) of the flour with the garlic and onion powders; set aside.

Heat the oil to 350°F (180°C) in a large, deep skillet—make sure there's enough to submerge the nuggets, or fill a deep fryer with oil as directed by the manufacturer. If you don't have a thermometer, you can test the oil by sticking a wooden chopstick or the end of a wooden spoon about 1 inch (2.5 cm) deep into the oil. If you see bubbles, the oil is hot enough for frying.

In a large bowl, stir the remaining cup (125 g) of flour into the beer. Dredge the corn nuggets in the spiced flour mixture, then in the beer mixture. Fry two or three at a time until golden brown, 3 to 5 minutes. Be careful; the corn can sometimes pop when it gets hot. Drain on paper towels before serving hot.

Note: If you're straight edge, don't worry—the alcohol burns off in the fryer, but you could always substitute nonalcoholic beer or seltzer water. Just ramp up the amount of seasoning you're using if you opt for bubbly water.

Kale Chips 5 Ways

Welcome to the world of kale chips! As with potato chips, you can make them in any flavor your heart desires. Unlike potato chips, eating a whole batch is a nutritional accomplishment, not a point of humiliation. If you can't eat the whole pile in one shot, store them loosely covered on your countertop to keep them crunchy for a few days.

Before you make any of these kale chips, wash and dry your kale and remove the ribs (that thick stem in the middle). Rip the leaves into bite-size pieces (they'll shrink as they cook, so I like to rip them into 2 to 3-inch (5 to 7.5 cm) pieces.

Low and slow cooking is the secret to a crispy chip, so I keep my oven door propped slightly open while I bake these and check on them often. Rotate the pans back to front and top to bottom to make sure all the leaves cook without burning.

Vaguely Asian

As an Italian-American who is often mistaken for Russian, I feel uncomfortable pinpointing the Asian cuisine that may have inspired this flavor. So I'll keep it vague.

Serves 4

Ingredients

½ teaspoon chili powder

½ teaspoon lemon pepper

1 bunch kale

1 tablespoon (15 ml) apple cider vinegar

1 ½ teaspoons sesame oil

1 ½ teaspoons freshly squeezed lime juice

1 clove garlic, minced

1 (½" [1.3 cm]) slice fresh ginger, peeled and minced

2 tablespoons sesame seeds

Directions

Preheat your oven to 200°F (93°C). In a small bowl, combine the chili powder and lemon pepper and set aside. Toss the kale with the vinegar, sesame oil and lime juice, then gradually add the dried spice mixture. Make sure each leaf is coated in spices. Add the garlic, ginger and sesame seeds, and give it a quick stir to evenly distribute.

Spread the kale in a single layer on lined baking sheets—you might need to scrape some ginger and garlic pieces from the bottom of the bowl. Place the kale in the oven and prop the door open. Bake for 10 minutes and check on the progress. Rotate the sheets as necessary. Keep baking in 10-minute increments until the kale is dry and crispy, 20 to 30 minutes.

Salt & Vinegar

As easy as it gets—if you're new to homemade kale chips, start here and note any of your oven's hot spots or weird quirks before you move on to a more complicated recipe.

Serves 4

Ingredients

1 bunch kale
2 tablespoons (30 ml) white vinegar
1 ½ teaspoons olive oil
Salt

Directions

Preheat your oven to 200°F (93°C). Gently massage the kale with vinegar and oil (try not to crush it) and place in a single layer on lined baking sheets. Sprinkle with salt, but go easy; you can always add more after baking. Place the kale in the oven and prop open the door. Bake for 10 minutes, then check on the progress. Rotate the sheets as necessary. Keep baking in 10-minute increments until the kale is dry and crispy, 20 to 30 minutes.

Radical Ranch

Tangy ranch chips are my all-time favorite, so I did the sweetest of all victory dances upon completing this recipe. If these chips also make you dance, please send me videos.

Serves 4

Ingredients

3 tablespoons (12 g) nutritional yeast
1 tablespoon (6.9 g) onion powder
1 tablespoon (9 g) garlic powder
2 teaspoons dried dill
1 bunch kale
2 tablespoons (30 ml) white vinegar
2 tablespoons (30 ml) freshly squeezed lemon juice
1 tablespoon (15 ml) olive oil
Salt and freshly ground black pepper

Directions

Preheat your oven to 200°F (93°C). In a small bowl, combine nutritional yeast, onion and garlic powders and dill and set aside. Toss the kale with the vinegar, lemon juice and olive oil, then gradually add the dried spice mixture. Make sure each leaf is coated in spices. You can also add some salt and pepper to taste.

Spread the kale in a single layer on lined baking sheets. Place the kale in the oven and prop the door open. Bake for 10 minutes and check on the progress. Rotate the sheets as necessary. Keep baking in 10-minute increments until the kale is dry and crispy, 20 to 30 minutes.

BBQ Kale Chips

You might be looking at this recipe and wondering if allspice is a typo, but believe me, it's the secret to an accurate BBQ chip flavor. Add more cayenne if you want a little hair on your chest.

Serves 4

Ingredients

1 bunch kale

1 tablespoon (15 ml) apple cider vinegar

1 ½ teaspoons olive oil

2 teaspoons paprika

1 teaspoon garlic powder

½ teaspoon onion powder

½ teaspoon allspice

¼ teaspoon cayenne pepper

¼ teaspoon dried thyme, crushed between your fingers

Salt and freshly ground black pepper

Directions

Preheat your oven to 200°F (93°C). In a small bowl, stir together the paprika, garlic and onion powders, allspice, cayenne pepper and thyme. In a large bowl, toss the kale with the vinegar and oil, then gradually add the dried spice mixture. Make sure each leaf is coated in spices. Add salt and pepper to taste.

Spread the kale in a single layer on lined baking sheets. Place the kale in the oven and prop the door open. Bake for 10 minutes and check on the progress. Rotate the sheets as necessary. Keep baking in 10-minute increments until the kale is dry and crispy, 20 to 30 minutes.

Dorneatos (Nacho Cheese)

The flavor of these kale chips lies somewhere between ranch and BBQ—cheesy, smoky and a touch spicy. Kick up the spice with a pinch of cayenne powder if you're into that sort of thing.

Serves 4

Ingredients

1 bunch kale
1 tablespoon (15 ml) olive oil
1 tablespoon (15 ml) white vinegar
3 tablespoons (12 g) nutritional yeast
1 teaspoon onion powder
1 teaspoon garlic powder
1 ½ teaspoons chili powder
¼ teaspoon dried oregano
Pinch each of salt and freshly ground black pepper

Directions

Preheat your oven to 200°F (93°C). In a small bowl, combine the nutritional yeast, onion and garlic powders, chili powder and oregano and set aside. Toss the kale with the oil and vinegar, then gradually add the dried spice mixture. Make sure each leaf is coated in spices. Add salt and pepper to taste.

Spread the kale in a single layer on lined baking sheets. Place the kale in the oven and prop the door open. Bake for 10 minutes and check on the progress. Rotate the sheets as necessary. Keep baking in 10-minute increments until the kale is dry and crispy, 20 to 30 minutes.

Stuffin' Muffins

My favorite part of holiday meals is stuffing (or "dressing," depending on who you ask). The problem with holidays, though, is there are only a few, and I want stuffing year-round. I made these muffins to enjoy a side of stuffing with just about any meal, any time of the year. They even make soup less boring!

Makes 12 muffins

Ingredients

2 tablespoons (28 g) vegan margarine

1 cup (150 g) corn kernels (fresh or frozen)

½ cup (50 g) chopped celery

1 small onion, finely chopped

1 cup (125 g) all-purpose flour

⅓ cup (67 g) sugar

1 tablespoon (2 g) dried sage

2 teaspoons baking powder

¾ teaspoon salt

Pinch of freshly ground black pepper

1 cup (170 g) stone-ground yellow cornmeal

⅓ cup (76 g) unhydrogenated vegetable shortening, plus more for pan

1 cup (235 ml) plain soy milk

¼ cup (60 g) blended silken tofu

Directions

Preheat your oven to 350°F (180°C) and coat a twelve-cup muffin pan with shortening.

Melt the margarine in a medium-size sauté pan over medium-high heat; add corn, celery and onion. Cook, stirring occasionally, until the corn and onion are softened, about 5 minutes.

In a medium-size bowl, whisk together the flour, sugar, sage, baking powder, salt and pepper. Stir in the cornmeal. Using a pastry blender (or a fork) cut in the shortening until the mixture resembles coarse meal. Add the soy milk, tofu and sautéed vegetables, stirring until just combined.

Scoop the batter into the prepared pan and bake for 18 to 20 minutes, until the tops are golden and a toothpick inserted in center comes out clean. Transfer to a wire rack to cool.

Crouching Cornbread, Hidden Broccoli

I think most parents are convinced, at least for a short while, that their toddlers are going to starve. How on Earth could a growing body possibly survive on little more than juice boxes and goldfish crackers? The fear of accidentally starving my child led me to creating this recipe, which disguises a few veggies as sweet, delicious cornbread. If you really want to get sneaky, add a bit of wheat germ or flaxseeds!

Makes 12 pieces

Ingredients

1 tablespoon (14 g) vegan margarine

1 cup (150 g) corn kernels (fresh or frozen)

1 medium-size broccoli crown

1 cup (125 g) all-purpose flour

⅓ cup (67 g) sugar

2 teaspoons baking powder

¾ teaspoon salt

1 cup (170 g) stone-ground yellow cornmeal

3 cup (76 g) unhydrogenated vegetable shortening, plus more for the pan

1 cup (235 g) soy milk

¼ cup (60 g) blended silken tofu

½ cup (55 g) shredded carrots

Directions

Preheat your oven to 350°F (180°C) and coat a twelve-cup muffin pan with shortening.

Melt the margarine in a medium-size sauté pan over medium-high heat; add the corn. Cook, stirring occasionally, until the corn is softened and some of the kernels are a light golden brown, about 5 minutes. Remove from the heat and set aside to cool slightly.

While that's cooling, steam the broccoli for about 2 minutes, until bright green and softened. Let cool slightly and chop into small pieces.

In a medium-size bowl, whisk together the flour, sugar, baking powder and salt. Stir in the cornmeal. Using a pastry blender (or a fork) cut in the shortening until the mixture resembles coarse meal. Add the soy milk, tofu, corn, broccoli and shredded carrots, stirring until just combined. Do not overmix!

Scoop the batter into the prepared pan and bake for 18 to 20 minutes, until the tops are golden and a toothpick inserted in center comes out clean. Transfer to a wire rack to cool. Yummy served warm, but just as good at room temperature.

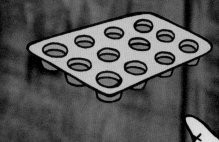

FOOD FIGHT!

BAKE AND DESTROY

Chapter 6

Tips, Tools and Magic Tricks

It's the worst when cookbook authors assume you have a kitchen full of fancy equipment and Wolfgang Puck's food budget. I'm writing this book in a small Chicago apartment with a regular old kitchen, so I tried to keep it real.

I kept it so real, in fact, that I sourced 95 percent of my ingredients from Andy's Fruit Ranch, a small grocery store right by my house. Every few days when I went back to stock up, the cashiers would compliment me on my ability to shop healthy on a budget—there are no Meyer lemons or truffle oil in this book, my friends.

As I developed recipes, I had two people in mind: My mom, who recently went vegetarian and lives in a not-so-veggie-friendly town; and my cousin Alison, who is also vegetarian but cooking and eating on a college student's budget. I regularly took surveys of my Facebook friends who live all over the world to gauge the availability of specialty ingredients, and adjusted recipes accordingly.

This chapter includes info on basic ingredients and equipment you'll need to get started, as well as some extra things you could pick up to make your life easier. Check out the Resources section for info on where to find some of the things you might not be able to source locally.

Ingredients

THE FLOUR POWER HOUR

These recipes call for all-purpose flour unless otherwise specified. But if you're cooking for people who are already keen on the idea of whole grains, feel free to substitute up to half of the flour in any of these recipes with whole wheat flour. I recommend white whole wheat flour and/or whole wheat pastry flour for dessert recipes. If you're new to the idea, but willing to try, start by replacing one-quarter of the flour with whole wheat. It's a good way to introduce whole grains into your diet without making your food taste like cardboard.

CUT ME SOME FLAXSEEDS

These wee seeds are high in omega-3 fatty acids and all-around good for you. You can grind them up and hide them in most cookies and muffins, or take advantage of their nutty flavor and throw them on top of salads. You can also use ground flaxseeds and a little water to replace eggs in many baking recipes! (See "Suck an Egg" below for more.) Purchase flaxseed meal if you don't feel like grinding the seeds yourself—but keep in mind that once ground, flaxseeds need to be stored in the refrigerator.

SUCK AN EGG

By now you've probably noticed that none of these recipes call for eggs. Very observant of you! In an effort to minimize cholesterol and maximize refrigerator space, I use other pantry staples in place of eggs. Here's a quick guide for replacing eggs in your other favorite recipes (each one replaces one egg):

- ½ banana, mashed

- ¼ cup (60 g) applesauce

- ¼ cup (60 g) blended silken tofu

- ¼ cup (60 g) plain, unsweetened nondairy yogurt

- 2 ½ tablespoons (17 g) ground flaxseeds + 3 tablespoons (45 ml) water

You can also use Ener-G Egg Replacer, although many people don't like the taste or texture of baked goods made with this.

Use your common sense when choosing an egg replacement—fruit will flavor your dish, so stick to desserts when using bananas or applesauce.

SUGAR COMA

I use old-fashioned white sugar in my desserts. I would rather have some sugar in moderation rather than artificial sweeteners that play tricks on your body and can leave a nasty aftertaste. If you'd like to cut back on processed white sugar, I recommend these all-natural alternatives:

Agave nectar: Use ⅔ cup (216 g) of agave for every 1 cup (200 g) of white sugar called for. Reduce other liquids in the recipe by ¼ cup (60 ml), or your batter will be too loose. To prevent burning, lower your baking temperatures by about 25°F (13°C) and slightly increase your baking time.

Maple syrup: Use ¾ cup (243 g) for every 1 cup (200 g) of sugar called for and reduce other liquids by 3 tablespoons (45 ml). For even baking, add ¼ teaspoon of baking soda for every 1 cup (317 g) of maple syrup. As with agave nectar, lower your baking temperatures by 25°F (13°C) to prevent overbrowning.

Stevia: Best used with bold flavors, such as coffee and chocolate, and even then, some people don't like the aftertaste. It's extremely sweet, so replace every 1 cup (200 g) of sugar with 1 teaspoon of powdered stevia or liquid concentrate. To make up for lost bulk in your recipe, add applesauce, apple butter or vegan soy yogurt.

What about honey? Silly bear, honey isn't vegan!

BETTER BELIEVE IT'S NOT BUTTER

I use Earth Balance Vegan Buttery Sticks in my recipes because they're nonhydrogenated, but there are now other vegan margarines on the market to experiment with. I also only used nonhydrogenated vegetable shortening in these recipes. Check out Tips and Tricks (page 183) for more shocking news about margarine!

NOT MILK?

I prefer unflavored, unsweetened nondairy milk—especially in savory recipes. I used plain soy milk in all of these recipes unless otherwise specified. You could also use almond milk, but I don't recommend rice milk as it lacks the body soy and almond milk offer, and coconut milk tends to make everything taste like coconut.

To make vegan buttermilk, add 1 teaspoon of white vinegar or lemon juice to 1 cup of soy milk and set aside to curdle for a few minutes.

TOFU

You've probably heard some people refer to tofu as a flavor sponge, because it takes on the flavors of whatever you marinate it with. There are just a few things you need to know about tofu before you start throwing it into everything you eat.

KNOW YOUR FU

Silken tofu is Japanese style; it's soft and squishy (even if you buy extra-firm) and comes packaged in water, or in aseptic containers that don't require refrigeration. For tofu beginners, it's best used as an egg replacement in baking, as an ingredient in dips and dressings or in smoothies.

Regular tofu has a drier, meatier texture, and comes packaged in water. It retains its shape, so it's great on a sandwich or in a stir-fry, but it can also be mashed and crumbled. Regular tofu can also be purchased premarinated, baked or fried in some stores.

Most recipes that call for tofu, including those in this book, specify which type of tofu you should use.

PRESS YOUR FU

Pressing your tofu is the first step to flavoring it. Before flavor can go in, the extra water must come out. Do this in four easy steps:

Slice open the tofu package and drain out the water. Cut the block of tofu width-wise into four slices.

Line a baking sheet with several layers of paper towels or clean kitchen towels, and place the tofu slices on top. Place more towels on top of the tofu, and put another baking sheet on top.

Place heavy objects on top of the upper baking sheet—books, a full teapot, whatever you have around. Leave it for at least 30 minutes—or, to really get the extra water out, move your whole contraption into the refrigerator and leave it overnight. (Not entirely necessary, but sometimes I do this if I'm thinking about it before I go to bed.)

Uncover, and you're ready to marinate. You can leave your tofu in big slabs, or cut it into smaller pieces.

FLAVOR YOUR FU

There are lots of ways to marinate tofu—from premade marinades you can get at the store, to homemade mixtures made with vegetable stock, soy sauce, vinegar or anything else you like. Just don't use oil-based marinades because the water still left in the tofu will prevent oily marinades from being absorbed.

FREEZE YOUR FU

For a really chewy, meaty texture, freeze your tofu after pressing out the water. Place pressed slabs or diced pieces in a resealable plastic bag and freeze them overnight. Let them thaw in the fridge before cooking, for a totally unique texture.

Technically, you don't *have* to cook tofu. Sometimes a couple of uncooked chunks of marinated tofu on top of a fresh salad can really hit the spot. But if you're hankering for some hot 'fu, here are some ways to achieve that:

Fried Fu: Toss marinated tofu into a resealable plastic bag containing ¼ cup of cornstarch (37 g), all-purpose flour (31 g) or cornmeal (42 g). Use a colander to shake off any excess coating, and panfry or stir-fry in a little oil.

Baked Fu: Place marinated slices of tofu on a baking sheet sprayed with cooking spray. Bake in a preheated 350°F (180°C) oven for 20 to 45 minutes, depending on how firm and chewy you like your tofu. If you're a first-timer, check on your tofu after 15 minutes, and flip it over while you're at it. Try different cook times for different textures.

Grilled Fu: You can grill tofu just as you would meat or vegetables. Just grease your grill with a little oil, and grill slabs of marinated tofu, until both sides have nice grill marks.

Tools

Aside from the usual mixing bowls, cooking sheets and measuring cups that all recipe books are going to assume you already own, there are a few tools you might want to pick up.

Food processor: I used mine a lot while writing this book, for everything from blending tofu to shredding carrots.

Silicone baking mats: These replace parchment paper and, in most cases, the need for cooking spray, so they save you money and cut back on kitchen waste. I have the expensive French version and the cheapo version and they work exactly the same way.

Donut pan: Available in mini and full-size. I prefer baking donuts over frying them. Baked donuts are healthier and they store better.

Whoopie pie pan: Technically, you can scoop whoopie pies onto parchment paper–covered cookie sheets, but I like the perfectly round results a special whoopie pie pan gives.

Mini muffin pan: I'm assuming you already own a standard muffin pan or two. Minis are a nice option for when you're cooking for a lot of people, or just to cut down portion sizes.

Pizza stone: Essential for making homemade pizzas. Pizza stones absorb excess moisture from your dough and help produce a firm, chewy crust.

Canoe pan: These pans bake little cakes shaped like a store-bought treat that rhymes with "minkie." To make your own canoe pans at home, shape heavy-duty aluminum foil around a cardboard toilet paper tube and remove the tube. Make as many foil pans as you need, and line them up on a rimmed baking sheet to fill and bake.

Salad spinner: I thought these were the stupidest things ever until I found one on clearance for five dollars and now I use it every day. It speeds up drying time on leafy greens while also taking up an absurd amount of space in my cupboard. Okay, maybe it is stupid, after all—but if you get one at your wedding shower, don't throw it away!

Kitchen scale: European recipes call for ingredients by weight, which is technically much more accurate than American measurements. I mainly use my kitchen scale to weigh out the amount of tofu I need when I buy it in large blocks, but it's pretty handy, so go ahead and put one on your birthday list.

Double boiler: Double boilers are the perfect tool for slowly, gently heating temperamental ingredients, such as chocolate—but don't bother buying one, because you can make one out of things you already own. All you need is a glass or nonreactive metal mixing bowl and a saucepan that the bowl fits on top of. The bowl should fit snugly, so steam gets trapped between the pan and the bowl when in use. To use, simmer a little water in the bottom pan, low enough not to touch the bowl, and place the bowl on top. Fill the bowl with whatever you're cooking or melting. Voilà! Double boiler action.

Weirdo Ingredients

Again, I tried to keep these limited because I know what it's like to get player-hated by a recipe that calls for a rare berry found only in the jungles of Africa. Thankfully, there is now a thing called the Internet that makes it easy to purchase things not readily available at your local supermarket, so if you can't locate these in your local grocery store (and don't forget to check out ethnic markets), then just check the web. (See Resources for more specific source info.)

Arrowroot starch: This thickener is similar to cornstarch, but different enough that it's worth adding to your pantry. It has a more neutral flavor than cornstarch, and works better with acidic liquids, such as citrus, to make clear gels and sauces.

Bragg Liquid Aminos: This product tastes like soy sauce (because it's made from soybeans) but contains less sodium, and the sodium it does contain is naturally occurring.

Jackfruit: These huge fruits (up to 80 pounds [36 k]!) come from Southeast Asia, where they've earned the nickname "tree mutton," thanks to the poultry-like texture of the young, unripe flesh. Look for young jackfruit in brine in Asian markets, or in the ethnic aisle at your grocery store. Don't use jackfruit in syrup for the recipes in this book, as it will be much too sweet.

Nutritional yeast: This deactivated yeast has a nutty, cheesy flavor, and therefore makes delicious dairy-free cheese and sauces. It can be pricey, but a good-size container will last you a long time. Look for it in the bulk bins at your favorite health food store.

White whole wheat flour: All the whole-grain goodness of whole wheat flour but with a lighter flavor, so you can sneak it into most recipes without offence.

Whole wheat pastry flour: Also known as graham flour, this is another whole-grain flour with a light flavor. It's milled from a soft wheat, so it's perfect for dessert baking, such as cookies, cakes, and piecrusts.

Tips and Terms

Just some general info that will help to make the kitchen a less scary place.

FRESH OR FROZEN

Fresh greens and vegetables are generally preferred over frozen, unless a recipe specifically calls for or gives the option of using frozen. Frozen fruit, however, is a good option when the fruit a recipe calls for is out of season. (Only use frozen bananas in smoothies, though, because you need to mash them up for baking.)

Oh, and if you're zesting a lemon, lime or orange, buy organic. The thick rind is where all the chemical nasties hide in nonorganic fruit.

TRUST NO ONE

There's a good chance your oven is lying to you. If you don't have an oven thermometer, cough up about five dollars and get one ASAP. I have yet to meet an oven that doesn't run 10°F to 20°F (5.6°C to 10°C) hot or cold, which can make a big difference in cook times.

I'LL CUT YOU

This book's cutting terminology made simple.

Chop: Cut food into bite-size pieces. You are not a food processor; take it easy.

Mince: Smaller than bite-size, but not super small.

Dice: Smaller than minced—cut food into tiny cubes.

Grate: Use a grater for this. Rub or scrape the food, breaking it down into small shreds. Most often done with ginger and citrus zest in this particular book.

FLAME ON

Your stove is talking; are you prepared to listen? Most stoves' knobs are marked with some sort of number system, from low to high heat. Low heat is best for simmering, high is for boiling. If a recipe calls for a medium flame, shoot for somewhere between the two. You should be able to eyeball it with a gas range, but US electric ranges can be tricky, so use those numbers as your guide. Medium-low would be around 3 to 4, whereas medium-high is 6 to 7.

EL GENERICO

In the early 2000s I started writing a zine titled *Accidentally Vegan*, in which I listed all the unintentionally vegan foods I'd discovered as a broke, lazy food-eater. But because I am so lazy, I never finished writing it. The spirit of this abandoned project lives on all over the Internet, with lots of new blogs and Tumblrs documenting vegan commercial products. In-the-know vegans skip the health food stores and look for generic versions of pantry staples in the regular grocery store, as they're more likely to contain nondairy alternatives.

Chocolate chips: Look for semisweet and scan the ingredients for milk or butter. Most generics I've found check out (though purists may wish to avoid nondairy chips whose label states they have been processed on the same equipment as milk products). Trader Joe's semisweet chips are also vegan at the time of publication, as are 365 (the house brand of Whole Foods), SunSpire and Enjoy Life vegan chips.

Graham crackers: As I write this, Nabisco Original Grahams are vegan, but also check out off-brand graham crackers and those found in health food stores.

Margarine: Contrary to popular belief, not all margarine is vegan—many contain some form of milk. Check out the ingredients next time you shop, but I can recommend Earth Balance and Becel Vegan to be sure.

Acknowledgments

I want to thank everyone involved in creating this book. Thanks to my agent Sally Ekus for talking me into writing a cookbook, and to William Kiester and Marissa Giambelluca for making it easy. Thank you to Celine Steen for your beautiful food styling and photography and to the whole Page Street Publishing team for working hard to make this book not-your-average cookbook. Thank you, Agnes Barton-Sabo for your hilarious illustrations, and to Amanda and Kristina Bourlotos for creating the Bake and Destroy logo and cover illustrations. Oh, and thanks to Sean Dorgan for taking pictures of me!

Thanks to my team of recipe testers: Lynne Rigazio-Mau (my mom), Alison Rigazio (favorite cousin), Lisa Simendinger (pastry chef loudmouth), and Nichelle Nicholes (plant-based derby girl).

The biggest thanks of all goes to my husband, Tony Slater, who was on Mr. Mom duty the whole time I was plugging away in the kitchen. *You're so cool!* (Also thanks to our son, Teno, for trying his hardest to be good while I was working.) Speaking of Teno, thanks so much to Leslie and Jo Ann for all your help with him and with taste-testing!

Thank you to my friends and family who cheered me on—CM Punk, Mike Edison, Amy Dumas, Matt Barnette, Thaddeus Mountain, Tony Loza, Joy Garcia-Roughton, Jessica Hallinan, Melisser Elliott, my sister Nina and my brother Aaron, my grandma and papa, my Uncle Dave and to all of my aunts, uncles, and cousins who inflate my ego by pretending like I am cool. I love you all.

And thank you to my dad, Dan Mau, who loved to cook and eat, and who taught me that the harder you work, the luckier you get. I love you and I miss you.

Resources

As a general rule of thumb, ethnic grocery stores and the ethnic aisle at your favorite major grocery store are great places to look for such things as tofu, jackfruit, and spring roll wrappers, as well as any specialty spices you might not spot in the baking aisle. Shop the bulk bins at your favorite health food or natural food stores for the best deals on nutritional yeast, raw nuts, oats, grains and so on. Oh, and cruise down the kosher aisle while you're at it and look for items marked "pareve," which means meat- and dairy-free. Note, however, that some pareve products do contain eggs and/or fish.

Baker's Catalogue at King Arthur Flour

bakerscatalogue.com

Flavor extracts, fancy flours, dark cocoa powder and other ingredients and tools for a well-stocked bakery. Also look for their products in the baking aisle.

Betty Turbo

etsy.com/shop/BettyTurbo

Artist Agnes Barton-Sabo's love of pop culture, pro-wrestling and food are evident in her work, which you can purchase as prints, greeting cards, pillows and more on Etsy. Oh, and she also illustrated this book!

Bob's Red Mill

bobsredmill.com

Nutritional yeast, dried beans, seeds . . . all kinds of magical things! You can find Bob's products in most well-stocked grocery stores, but if you prefer to shop naked, order online.

Circa Ceramics

circaceramics.com

Officially the cutest ceramic items on the entire Internet, and in this book! Bright colors, quirky screenprints and craftsmanship that will last a lifetime. My kitchen is full of Circa Ceramics and yours should be, too.

Food Fight! Vegan Grocery

foodfightgrocery.com

Located in Portland, Oregon, Food Fight! is a magical land where you don't even need to read the labels because everything is vegan. From staples to supplements, they have it all.

Girl's Town

hey-amanda.com

Amanda Bourlotos designed my website (BakeandDestroy.com) as well as my official logo. I highly recommend her services to anyone looking to make over a blog, e-commerce site, or who wants some help with branding. She's also a fantastic writer and photographer, so there.

Herbivore Clothing

herbivoreclothing.com

With their plethora of vegan-themed T-shirts (my favorites are riffs on Motorhead and Powell Skateboards designs) Herbivore has everything you need to be a cool-looking vegan.

Layer Cake Shop

layercakeshop.com

All the cute cupcake wrappers, decorating tips and packaging supplies a baker could want. Plus, lots of vegan sprinkles and food coloring options.

Obsessive Compulsive Cosmetics

occmakeup.com

If, like me, you don't step foot into the kitchen until you have your face on, you're going to love this 100 percent vegan, cruelty-free cosmetics line. NSFW Lip Tar is my official red lip color. You heard it here first.

Pangea Vegan Store

veganstore.com

Gelatin-free marshmallows, baking mixes, gummy candies and more are just a click away, thanks to this one-stop vegan shop.

Vegan Cuts

vegancuts.com

This site carries a wide variety of vegan products from personal care to snacks—but the coolest feature for newbie vegans or curious shoppers is the Snack Box.

Index

About the Author

NATALIE SLATER is the creator and writer of Bake and Destroy, "the food blog equivalent to a punch in the throat." She served as a judge on Food Network's *Cupcake Wars* and her recipes have appeared in *Bust Magazine*, *Time Out Chicago* and several online publications. Natalie resides in Chicago, Illinois, with her husband and son.